DIVIDE & RULE

South Africa's
BANTUSTANS
by
Barbara Rogers

International Defence & Aid Fund
104 Newgate Street EC1
Fully revised and enlarged edition 1980

First published 1976

Revised and enlarged edition 1980

The International Defence and Aid Fund for Southern Africa has the following objects:—

1. To aid, defend and rehabilitate the victims of unjust legislation and oppressive and arbitrary procedures;

2. To support their families and dependants;

3. To keep the conscience of the world alive to the issues at stake.

ISBN No. 0 904759 40 7

Contents

Introduction

Previous editions of this publication have focused on the realities of South Africa's Bantustan policy, attempting to put into perspective the South African Government's claims to be providing true homelands for the African majority. Since the last edition, in 1976, the Government has announced the "independence" of three Bantustans, the Transkei, BophuthaTswana and Venda, with a massive propaganda effort to sell the idea to world opinion. The attempt has been one of South Africa's most conspicuous failures. Not one country has recognised either the Transkei, BophuthaTswana or Venda.

The South African answer has been to change the terminology used in the administration of Africans—"Plural Relations" and "Co-operation and Development" instead of Bantu Affairs, "independent national entities" and "Black States" rather than Bantu homelands. Public relations presentations have stressed the official claim to be "developing" the Bantustans. Behind the public facade, however, there have been a proliferation of emergency proclamations removing most remaining rights inside the Bantustans, together with deportations to them of urban and rural Africans and the wholesale removal of many Africans already there whose official classification does not fit into the grand design of "independent" Bantustans.

At the same time, countries which have formally refused to recognise South Africa's policy are quietly promoting the official nominees heading the Bantustans as African "leaders". They are frequently feted in North America and Western Europe, and used to promote South African objectives such as the continued flow of investment into the Republic, sometimes directly into the Bantustans themselves.

In preparing this new edition of *Divide and Rule*, the reporting from inside the Bantustans of African journalists from *The World* (now banned) and *The Post* has been of major importance. The future of newspapers catering for Africans is under constant threat from the South African Government; it is vital that outsiders be aware of how crucial they are in revealing the realities behind South Africa's ubiquitous propaganda. This new edition has drawn on considerably better and more detailed reporting than previous editions, mainly due to these two papers.

CHAPTER 1

Bantustans in Theory

Historical background

Statements from the South African Government about the Bantustans frequently stress that they have a historical basis as the traditional tribal homelands of
the "Bantu".* A standard school text book, for example, claims:
"These were the areas of South Africa where the Bantu had always lived and
which belonged to them."[1]
The historical and archaeological evidence is against such an interpretation, indi-
cating that Africans occupied the whole of South Africa well before the Europeans
arrived. There are traces of long-established African settlements, including copper
and other mines, in many areas now occupied by "white" farms and cities.[2] From
the very beginning of colonial settlement and occupation of the area, Africans
resisted the colonists' encroachment on their land. Jan van Riebeeck, the leader of
the first party of colonists, wrote to his directors in Holland in 1652:
"The prisoner . . . having been asked the reason why they had caused us this
trouble, declared for no other reason than that they saw that we kept in possession the best lands, and grazed our cattle where they used to do so, and that
everywhere with houses and plantations we endeavoured to establish ourselves
so permanently as if we intended never to leave again, but take permanent possession of this Cape land (which had belonged to them during all the centuries)
for our sole use . . ."[3]
The idea of establishing "native reserves", in which the Africans could be confined and which they would leave only in order to serve the whites, is almost as old
as the European occupation of South Africa. For example, one of the earliest acts
of the Volksraad, the People's Assembly of the new Boer Republic of Natal established in 1838, was to legislate for their customary distinction between themselves
and their chattels, the Africans. The Africans had no right to be in the settled parts
of the Boer Republic at all, except as servants of white people, and then were not
permitted to own land, firearms or horses, to participate in the political process, or
to be at large without passes signed by white employers. In 1841 it was decided that
no more than five African families could remain as labour tenants on each farm,
and that all "surplus" Africans should be placed in a certain area to which they

---

*Terminology is continually changing. The word "Bantu", official designation of Africans for many years,
took on a highly derogatory meaning resented by the people concerned. Officialdom is now changing to
the word "Blacks" for Africans only, which is confusing since the original sense of this, as used by the
Black Consciousness movement, for example, covered all groups—African, Asian, Coloured,
Chinese—hitherto known as "non-whites".

were to be sent by persuasion if possible, by force if necessary. This was not actually put into effect; it was the British, who took over shortly afterwards, who established the network of scattered reserve areas that now form the basis of the KwaZulu bantustan.[4]

The Transkei was conquered at a rather later date, and was maintained more or less intact by the British although with a much reduced land area, in order to provide a rational administrative entity which would be a source of what was then becoming an essential item in the white economy: migrant labour for the mines. The discovery by the whites of South Africa's great mineral wealth (known and worked for centuries by the Africans) coincided with the approximately 20 years when the Transkei was being absorbed into the Cape Colony, and a booming "get rich quick" amorality prevailed about the exploitation of South Africa's human as well as mineral resources. The British administration's "native policy" was dominated by the demand for cheap labour for the mines, and it therefore imposed a hut tax which forced thousands of Africans into the mines in order to obtain cash to pay the tax.[5] The hut tax is still in force in the Transkei and other bantustans, in spite of the inability of the population to achieve a basic subsistence level, let alone a cash surplus for paying taxes. The historian De Kiewiet has concluded:

"The congestion of the reserves, the backwardness of their methods, the exhaustion of their resources . . . (accounted) for the departure each year of a high proportion (50 per cent by 1925) of the able-bodied men to earn money as labourers . . . The natives were the victims of too few acres."[6]

In 1916 the Beaumont Commission reported on the prospects for an equitable division of land among the races, and concluded that this was no longer feasible:

"It is in fact far too late in the day to define large compact areas or to draw bold lines of demarcation; for . . . lands solely occupied by Natives are, with the exception of the Transkeian Territories, scattered in all directions and hopelessly intermixed with the lands owned and occupied by Europeans."[7]

The ideal of territorial segregation is not new, therefore, and from the very beginning there was agreement that the policy was designed for the requirements of the white economy. It was adopted and refined by the present-day rulers of South Africa as the most convenient system whereby Africans who are not directly contributing to white prosperity can be excluded from the rich zone, and not become burdens upon its resources; at the same time, by limiting the land and resources available to the poverty-stricken reserve areas, the able-bodied would be forced to leave them in order to find employment in white enterprises. The basic concept of separation of black men from their wives and families for the convenience of employers was also firmly established, rationalising the payment of wages so low that they could not support the wage-earner's dependants. The controls were not, however, sufficient to prevent a considerable degree of urbanisation of the African population dating from the mid-nineteenth century, a phenomenon which was simultaneous with the great movement towards urbanisation and industrialisation in Europe. It was left to the post-World War II Nationalist government in South Africa to attack the basis of this urban African population and to force the regression of African employment patterns back towards migrant labour on a mass scale.

Nationalist party policy: Bantustans and migrant labour

The idea of establishing "native reserves" for groups of people subject to systematic encroachment on their land is not unique to South Africa—although it is here that the concept is taken to its logical conclusion of mass deportation with a whole accompanying ideology to rationalise the separation of people along purely racial lines. European settlers in the United States, Canada and Australia all confined indigenous people, who regarded the land as rightfully theirs, to small areas of it. Although rationalised as "ancestral lands" or homelands, these reservations have in practice been the areas least wanted by the new settlers.

The most thorough-going example of the ideology of racial segregation is probably that prepared by the Nazis in their detailed plans for Africa under the Third Reich; the theory derives in turn from the South African "native reserve" policy. One of the German war aims was to take over the French and British colonies in Africa, sharing authority on that continent only with the South African Nationalists. The plans assumed the establishment of whites in the African colonies as the "Master Race", which would have no contact with blacks outside the sphere of work; however, the colonised people would support the white supremacist Reich by the provision of manual labour on a vast scale. The Nazi Ministry of Justice prepared draft legislation in 1940 under which the Reich could assign certain areas to the black inhabitants. If for any reason the colonial administration decided to restore these areas to the Reich, the blacks could be moved elsewhere. It would be a criminal offence for Africans to refuse work to which they were directed—which it has been effectively in South Africa ever since the establishment of a national network of "native reserves" in 1894. As a 1939 report to the Nazi Ministry of Justice stressed, quoting the South African experience, the purpose of the reserves was to give blacks an essentially economic function in serving the white economy as and when required by the Reich.[8]

In South Africa, documents have recently been published which indicate that the hitherto secret society, the Afrikaner Broederbond, was thinking along similar lines to the Nazi Party in Germany during the 1930s. The first Broederbond statement on race policy was in fact devoted to the idea of a comprehensive network of native reserves. The secret circular, in 1933, stated *inter alia* :

"Total segregation should not be only the ideal, but the immediate practical policy of the State. The purchase and separation of suitable and adequate areas for habitation by natives' families, and tribes living on farms and smaller reserves, should take place at any cost.

"The opportunity should be provided for different tribes to gather in separate areas. Then it should be made compulsory for these groups of natives to return to these areas."[9]

The policy is embodied in the segregation policies put into effect by the Nationalist Party after it gained power in 1948. Their election manifesto stated: "The Bantu in the urban areas should be regarded as migratory citizens not entitled to political or social rights equal to those of whites."

In 1950 both the Dutch Reformed Church and the South African Bureau of Racial Affairs (SABRA), the Afrikaners' intellectual establishment, came out in support of a policy of territorial and political separation of Africans from whites. The first Nationalist Prime Minister, Dr. D. F. Malan, introduced a note of economic self-interest in his response, saying that total separation was a valid ideal, but had to be put aside as "impractical under present circumstances. Our whole economic structure is to a large extent based upon non-white labour."[10]

It was Dr. Verwoerd (Prime Minister 1958-66) who proved the leading innovator in the ideology of "separate development," which is how he named the policy of *apartheid*. He was very much concerned about South Africa's image in the world, and threat of decolonisation in the rest of Africa. He laid great stress on separating the races, "separation in the political sphere at any rate."[11] There were many pressures, including the unrest of 1960-1 and the international revulsion at the Sharpeville massacre; the panic flight of capital from South Africa; and the isolation felt with the enforced withdrawal of South Africa from the Commonwealth in 1961.

In 1962 Verwoerd launched his counter-attack on the critics:

"I believe that these people (the Africans) should be given their own States as they desire . . . I have confidence in the mass of our Bantu, with the exception of a small group of agitators. I believe that they will see what is taking place in the rest of Africa, and this will strengthen the bonds between us, rather than lead to their joining up with foreign countries, which will result in conflict and chaos . . . We are trying to establish well-disposed little black neighbouring States and to safeguard them from such dangers by being prepared to render all kinds of services to them."[12]

In 1961 Dr. Verwoerd frankly admitted that "in the light of the pressure being exerted on South Africa," the Government would create through the Bantustans, "a form of fragmentation which we would not have liked if we were able to avoid it, thereby buying the white man his freedom and the right to retain domination in what is his country"[13] The fragmentation subsequently became a major element in the policy, involving as it did an arbitrary division of the old reserves along "tribal" lines as determined by the government; the process inevitably served to increase friction among Africans over land and other issues, and to deflect some of their energies away from attacking the central government towards concentrating on a number of separate entities whose visible chiefs were from among their own people.

Some observers believed that Dr. Verwoerd was speeding up and extending the political development of the Transkei largely to provide a model for the "separate development" of South West Africa (now known as Namibia). Ovambo chiefs and headmen were taken to see the Transkei; and elaborate testimony about it was laid before the International Court of Justice as a significant pattern for the future of South West Africa.[14]

Dr. Verwoerd, announcing self-government for the Transkei in 1962, said:
"This should strongly counteract the international animosity and suspicion which have such a detrimental effect on our economy. For this reason it will pay us to incur such expenditure. It is also worth a great deal to us if we can create for ourselves peaceful neighbours . . . who will not look to others for assistance."[15]

The Tomlinson Commission, appointed in the early 1950s to draw up a blueprint for the bantustan policy, foresaw that to make these territories economically viable would need massive infusions of capital and radically different policies towards Africans by providing employment in the bantustans. The Commission concluded that this was an immense task requiring an act of faith on the part of white South Africans:
"The choice is clear. Either the challenge must be accepted, or the inevitable consequences of the integration of the Bantu and European population groups into a common society, must be endured."[16]

Professor Tomlinson himself has subsequently condemned the government for its failure to implement the Commission's recommendations.[17] However, government statements sometimes give the impression that the Tomlinson challenge is being taken up. For example, Mr. M. C. Botha, former Minister of Bantu Administration and Development, has preached, "If it is something that must be done, and it is the right thing to do, then it is no sacrifice." He was announcing a Bill to remove many Africans from urban areas,[18] which, as he repeatedly stressed, is an idea that "should become an obsession with all of us."[19]

On the issue of independence there has been a definite shift in the official viewpoint. As recently as 1969 Mr. Botha was saying that the homelands would get their independence only at the turn of the century.[20] However, soon after his return from a visit to Europe in June 1970 Prime Minister Vorster initiated a radical switch in emphasis and announced that economic viability was no longer a prerequisite for political independence: "Each black State is free to come and tell parliament that it wants to be on its own." The decision was seen as a direct result of Mr. Vorster's visit to Malawi and Europe, where he was told by the South African ambassadors that the country's international position was becoming increasingly difficult to defend, and that some gesture should be made to facilitate the efforts of South Africa's friends to improve the image.[21]

Concern for South Africa's image abroad has led to rapid changes in terminology, if not in substance. The Department of Bantu Affairs and Development (BAD) became the Department of Plural Relations in 1978 and the Department of Co-operation and Development in 1979. Even the term "homelands", originally a euphemism for the bantustans, has been officially dropped: Dr. C. P. Mulder, who was Minister of Plural Relations, in 1978 declared that "a negative connotation is given to the word" and that homelands would in future be known as "self-governing states" or sometimes as "fatherlands".[22] The current official term now seems to be "Black States" or sometimes "emerging black nations." The policy, however, remains the same as originally prescribed by the Broederbond in 1933. The chairman of the Broederbond, Professor Gerrit Viljoen, said in his 1976 address that one of the main tasks for the future was:

"Effective and continuous implementation of our homeland policy so that the aim we seek can be achieved—the establishment of existence potential and therefore political homes for the majority of black people in their own homelands or states in order to form the basis of the maintenance of political power by whites in the so-called white country."[23]

The question of land

Although official Nationalist Party ideology has been in force only since 1948, the actual areas allocated to the bantustans remain those of the reserves which were least wanted by the white settlers over the years. They are widely scattered parcels of land, many of them no larger than a single farm, constituting about one-eighth of the total land area of the Republic. Current land allocation objectives got no further than the 1936 Trust and Land Act, a piece of legislation based on the 1913 Land Act which was based on the results of the colonial conquest and the robbery of the African people's land. The 1936 Act established what were already *de facto* African reserves as legal entities, with the intention of adding some more land, some of it in small parcels unrelated to the existing reservation areas. The Act was passed in order to facilitate the two-thirds majority the government of the time had wanted in order to remove Africans from the common voters' roll in the Cape. Total reserve area was planned as 6.21 million hectares, about 13.8% of the land area of South Africa.[24]

The 1936 Act remains the yardstick for land allocation to the bantustans despite desperate appeals from the bantustan chiefs who are trying to make sense of the policy. Chief Mangope of BophuthaTswana spoke for them all when he said:

"We reject outright the attempts to make the 1936 Land Act the basis of settling the issue. It was introduced to solve the then "Native Problem". In no way did the law claim or intend to provide additional areas for future independent sovereign States. (It) has no relevance whatsoever in respect of homeland consolidation negotiations."[25]

Both the expansion of existing area and the shifting of the bantustan boundaries, involving the deportation of large numbers of Africans, are issues of primary concern to the bantustan Chief Ministers, and they have frequently protested at the outrages of "consolidation" plans being imposed on them without even the pretence of consultation. This is discussed in more detail in Chapter 6. To each outburst, the government has responded with an attitude close to contempt. Mr. M. C. Botha, addressing himself to vociferous demands on land for the Transkei in 1972, informed Chief Matanzima and "all the Bantu peoples of South Africa":

" . . . if they think they can get more land than was allocated to the Bantu in the 1936 Act, by coupling it to independence, then they need not come and discuss it; they would be wasting their time and ours."[26]

The policy was reiterated by Mr. Vorster in April 1973, and on several subsequent occasions.[27] The impatience of the Government with demands for more land is obvious. Mr. M. C. Botha warned in 1972:

"A country's administration should be aimed at achieving what is practical and possible rather than at pursuing illusions."[28]

In 1974 Mr. Botha repeated the official line:

"We as the givers must determine what land should be given and it is not for those to receive to point out what land they should have."[29]

In particular he stressed that viable centres of economic activity could never be included in the bantustans. Replying to suggestions that the town of Pietersburg be included in a bantustan, he said it was too valuable; the budget for buying the remaining land owed under the 1936 Act was quite inadequate for buying a viable urban centre.[30]

The anomaly of pursuing a full-scale segregation policy on the basis of an old piece of legislation never intended to provide for "independent" bantustans with a single consolidated piece of territory has been disturbing the purists among the Afrikaner élite. Professor Carel Boshoff, chairman of SABRA, said in 1978:

"The 1936 Land Act was not aimed at consolidation but at providing land to accommodate numerous small tribes still in a 'pre-national' stage of development. The present consolidation programme, initiated in 1973, was an important step forward, but it is not the final step. For all practical purposes a further stage, consolidating the homelands into single territorial entities, will have to follow."[31]

The government, however, has refused to provide the land, or consolidate the different areas, to a degree commensurate with the ideology. In fact, over 40 years after the passage of the 1936 Land Act, the country is not even within sight of completing the land purchases envisaged in the Act. On the contrary, much of the land previously nominated as African reserve areas has been subject to removal of the African owners and sale to whites, under the so-called "black spot" removal policy. At the end of 1977, nearly 800,000 hectares of the quota lands had still not been bought, and another 54,000 hectares were owed because of the removal of "black spots".[32] Instead of the 13.8% of South Africa which the 1936 Act stipulated—itself grossly inadequate—the actual territory of the bantustans as of the end of 1977 was only 11.9%. Moreover, even if the price of land remained the same, an unlikely event, the official budget for purchasing land would allow the 1936 target to be met only in another ten years.[33] However, the budget for land purchase and consolidation is being reduced rather than increased; the 1978 budget, at R35 million, was R15 million less than the previous year's.[34] Toward the end of the year Deputy Minister Dr. Hartzenburg was having to renege on firm commitments to buy farms in key areas: "I have no money available and will not have any money available next year to buy out all the farms."[35] Promises to consolidate some of the bantustan areas by 1985 by buying extra land, made in 1975,[36] were being quietly dropped because of lack of funds. Instead, in early 1979 officials were beginning to plan consolidation by massive "swaps" of white and

11

reserve land with only minor additions—perhaps as little as between 4% and 5% of the remaining 1936 quota—at minimal financial cost. Such a policy would, however, entail large population removals from the crowded reserve areas, at considerable human cost.[37] Dr. Hartzenburg officially announced in September 1978 that despite pressure for the purchase or allocation of more land to the bantustans, the government would not go beyond the provisions of the 1936 Land Act; consolidation could take place only on the basis of an exchange of land. He appealed to Afrikaner intellectuals not to continue drawing up maps and plans for consolidation and enlargement of the bantustans, which he claimed would kill their "development" and political stability.[38]

In the latter part of 1979 the South African Prime Minister, Mr. P. W. Botha, intimated that the government was considering amendments to the 1936 Land Act.

The Chairman of the government's Commission of Inquiry into the Consolidation of the Homelands, Mr. Hennie van der Walt, speaking at the Transvaal Congress of the Nationalist Party, stated that he would be proposing changes to the 1936 Land Act. He said his changes aimed to make the "independent black states" more viable:

"The Commission cannot meaningfully consolidate the national black states without exceeding the provisions of the 1936 Act. We must be prepared to admit that to each other if we are serious about the constellation of states and about economic viability and separate freedom of the black states."[39]

In September 1979 the Johannesburg *Sunday Express* reported that "far-reaching land consolidation proposals . . . (involving) the mass removals of thousands of blacks and whites" would be recommended by the van der Walt commission. It also reported:

"The proposals concern the consolidation of 6-piece BophuthaTswana into one block. If they are accepted by the government, the homeland's new boundaries will stretch from Pretoria in the east to the Botswana border in the west . . . The Commission, chairman H. D. van der Walt said, would investigate consolidation for all homelands, but had been asked to give priority to BophuthaTswana."[40]

Further details of the Commission's recommendations revealed by the *Express* were that: huge tracts of land at present falling within BophuthaTswana would be "exchanged" with South Africa in order to consolidate the "white corridors" involved in the proposal; white farmers would be encouraged to stay in BophuthaTswana (in other words the change would be in many ways nominal); apart from Mafeking, no towns should be incorporated in the Bantustans; and that BophuthaTswana should forfeit its land at ThabaNchu in the Orange Free State and at Taunga in the Cape.

A few weeks earlier the Prime Minister and Minister of Defence, Mr. P. W. Botha, made it clear that the reason behind such proposals was the better protection of the *status quo*, not a move away from it. Addressing a Nationalist Party rally in the Transvaal, Mr. Botha asked his audience:

"Is the 1936 Land Act such a holy cow that we cannot change it in the interests of the safety of South Africa? I am not prepared to choose such a holy cow above the safety of South Africa."

He continued to say that land was scarce and South Africa could not give away land as if it were "Father Christmas."[41]

Whether the recommended changes are actually put into practice remains to be seen. However, it seems likely that any such changes would not add significantly to the land area of the bantustans, since they will be done on an exchange basis. In fact the bantustans could lose land in effect since their control over newly incorporated "white" farmland would be merely nominal.

CHAPTER 2

Bantustans and Official
Control over Urban Africans

Reserves of migrant labour

The bantustan policy is important for the whole African population in South Africa, and not by any means only confined to those people living in them or in the process of deportation there. What goes on inside these areas, and the relationship between them including the divisive issue of "independence", forms the major subject matter of this book. However, it is important to place it in the context of the government's policy towards urban Africans, the majority of the African people and perhaps the most important group in the whole of South Africa, from a political and economic point of view. For it is they who provide the cheap, rightless labour force for the South African economy, the basis of the *apartheid* system.

Despite the frequent claims that the bantustans provide a homeland for all Africans, and the imposition of bantustan citizenship on all African children born in South Africa, the planners are in fact well aware of the fact that this is a convenient fiction. Official statements on the topic of migrant labour demonstrate the essential pragmatism (and the cynicism) of the separate development policy when it comes to the economic self-interest of the white minority in power. As early as 1922, the Stallard Commission was reporting that an African:

".. . should only be allowed to enter the urban areas, which are essentially the white man's creation, when he is willing to enter and to minister to the needs of the white man, and should depart therefrom when he ceases so to minister."[1]

In effect, with South Africa an industrial nation with a long-standing African population in the towns and cities going back several generations and with no contacts with any of the old reserves, the policy means removing this entire population, millions of people; or removing their rights so that they can be deported, arrested, transported to camps and settlements, or forced to work. It also means the forcible separation of women from men, and children from parents; women in particular are regarded as "superfluous appendages" of men and increasingly shipped off to the bantustans or the transit camps where they are expected to maintain children, old people, the sick and handicapped. The men are in the towns for the sole purpose of serving the whites. Mr. M. C. Botha, Minister of Bantu Affairs, told the white House of Assembly in 1967:

"It must be understood very fundamentally that the Bantu who are working in the industries in South Africa on the basis of our policy . . . are not there on an integrationary basis . . . to become equal workers, equal entrepreneurs or equal partners."[2]

The idea was reinforced by Prime Minister John Vorster in 1968:

"It is true that there are blacks working for us. They will continue to work for us for generations, in spite of the ideal we have to separate them completely. Surely we all know that? . . .

"The fact of the matter is this: We need them, because they work for us . . . but the fact that they work for us can never — if one accepts this as one's own criterion one will be signing one's own death sentence now — entitle them to claim political rights. Not now, nor in the future. It makes no difference whether they are here with any degree of permanency or not . . ."[3]

The principle was elaborated by Mr. Froneman, Deputy Minister of Justice, Mines and Planning: the basis of all African labour was to be made migratory, even if the workers concerned were fully urbanised:

"We are trying to introduce (the) migratory labour pattern as far as possible in every sphere. That is in fact the entire basis of our policy as far as the white economy is concerned, namely a system of migratory labour."[4]

He then specified the conditions under which African labour could be used without conflicting with the ideology of separate development: the African labour force must not be domiciled in the white sector, or obtain citizenship or economic rights there — in other words, it must not grow to unmanageable proportions, and control measures must be applied at all times; and it must not be used to the detriment of the white labour force.[5] He emphasized the general need for African workers to be present in white areas:

"Both for their own sakes and for the sake of the white economy. Without them it would be impossible to maintain the essential growth rate . . ."[6]

Mr. Froneman's statement that the actual number of Africans was unimportant to the policy of separate development caused great dissension in the Nationalist Party, especially those with "idealistic concepts" of complete territorial *apartheid*. Mr. Froneman hastened to explain:

"I said emphatically that numbers definitely matter if they indicate the extent of integration, and that superfluous Bantu ought to be removed because their presence in the white homeland is not justified and promoted integration."[7]

To resolve the dilemma, it is essential to the Bantustan policy that there be large-scale removals of Africans who are not working for the whites, or "superfluous appendages" of those who are, at the same time as there is a general trend toward increased use of African labour in "white" industry. Mr. Botha has summarised the policy thus:

"As far as I am concerned the ideal condition would be if we could succeed in due course in having all Bantu present in the white areas on a basis of migratory labour only."[8]

And Mr. Vorster, answering questions in the House of Assembly as to whether it was still policy "to reduce the numbers of Bantu in the urban areas regardless of the consequences," challenged the opposition:

"Whoever said it was our policy to reduce the numbers of Bantu regardless of the consequences? We said we would like to reduce them and were doing our best to do so, but we said at all times we would not disrupt the South African economy."[9]

In response to the contradictions involved in a permanent African labour force in the urban areas when in theory they have no homes there, new townships are being set up some distance away from the employment centres, and labelled as belonging to one of the bantustans. This new development obviously makes nonsense of any attempt to consolidate the patches of land of each bantustan, creating as it does new patches, often with no geographical connection with the others at all. With the aid of these, and new townships built on the edge of some bantustans not too far from a town, some migrant labourers are being re-labelled "commuters", travelling long distances every day from a camp relabelled to fit the ideology. Dr. Hartzenberg, Deputy Minister of Development, told the House of Assembly in March 1978 that there would be high priority given to the increase of commuting — although at the same time money to subsidise the grossly inadequate bus service was "difficult to acquire" and it would be increasingly difficult to get such funds.[10] The chairman of the East Rand Bantu Board, which controls the workers of the major industrial area, has said that the "bantustan" townships in his area should not be regarded as normal towns but as labour reservoirs, appendages of the white towns."[11]

The trend is for the government and its agents to increase greatly their control over African workers, bantustan policies being a major instrument to this end. The national president of the Black Sash, a largely white women's organisation specialising in the problems of Africans in the towns, has described migrant labour — and its new variant, commuting — as an "unbelievable horror". The law enabled white officials to determine what work an African could do, and where; to attempt something else was illegal. Coercion was particularly obvious in the case of farm labour. She observed that because of the desperate need for jobs and the high level of government control, the bantustans could be forced to ask "voluntarily" for an independence which they had always opposed, in order to avoid a freeze on recruitment in their areas and therefore enormous numbers of unemployed and hungry people. The speaker, Mrs. Sheena Duncan, reminded her audience that certain privileges had already been promised to Transkei "citizens" by way of employment, housing and hospitals in the urban areas.[12]

The citizenship issue, whereby the entire African population is to be registered as belonging to an independent bantustan "nation" to the exclusion of all citizenship rights in South Africa, is central to the current policy. As the pace of "bantustanisation" increases, and pressures for the bantustans to accept "independent" status mount, it is in this area that people are being most directly affected. The white nationalist dream of a labour force without any rights whatever in the area where they live, the centres of employment, is becoming a reality by means of the "independent" bantustans.

The citizenship issue

A Broederbond circular of 1976, elaborating strategy for a previously outlined "masterplan for white survival", deals in detail with the removal of rights from urban Africans through the pursuit of an accelerated bantustan policy:

"It must be said candidly that there is no alternative to the policy of multi-national development in South Africa . . . The will and determination to make it succeed must be not only a slogan but a life philosophy . . . One stipulation remains paramount and that is that economic co-operation (with the homelands) and economic interdependence can be developed to full advantage only if political power has been finally divided and is accepted as such by black and white, especially by those black communities still relatively permanent in the white homeland . . . Those who do not willingly fall in with this cardinal precept must be compelled to do so in their own interests . . . Anyone who rejects the highest honour and right of every individual on earth, to be governed by himself . . . must be prepared to accept the dishonourable status of enslavement and the conditions accompanying it."[13]

Dr. Connie Mulder, speaking as Minister of Bantu Administration, introduced the 1978 Bantu Homelands Citizenship Amendment Bill by explaining:

"If our policy is taken to its logical conclusion as far as the Black people are concerned, there will be not one Black man with South African citizenship."[14]

Since 1970, following passage of the Bantu Homelands Citizenship Act, every African in the country is classified as a homeland citizen. Until 1976, they had a form of dual citizenship under which they remained also citizens of the Republic. The big change came with the "independence" of Transkei on 26 October 1976; from this date, everybody with "Xhosa" stamped in their reference book (better known as their pass book) lost their South African citizenship, unless specifically listed as belonging to the other "Xhosa" bantustan, Ciskei. There was no legal way for the people affected to recover their rights in South Africa. The same thing happened to all those classified as "Tswana", when BophuthaTswana became "independent" on 6 December 1977. In cases of doubt (for example, where one parent was "Tswana" and the other some other category) a person is invariably registered as Tswana; in this and other respects the Tswana legislation is even more severe than the earlier Transkei Act. The terminology is also very vague; for example, it is not specified exactly which African languages are to be considered related to Tswana and therefore classifying those who speak of them as "Tswanas". [15] The immediate impact of the new legislation was overwhelming confusion, with arbitrary official decisions being taken which irrevocably deprived people of whatever rights they had in South Africa. There were many reports of compulsion being used to force many people who denied any link with Transkei to accept the official papers.[16]

The "independence" of the Trankei and BophuthaTswana has meant that six million people have lost their South African citizenship — more than half of whom do not have a home of any kind in either territory.

The implications of the new laws were not adequately appreciated when they came into effect, according to Sheena Duncan. She has stressed that there is no need for overt compulsion; none of the people affected has to make any formal application for Transkeian or BophuthaTswana citizenship as "they already have had it thrust upon them whether they like it or not." Most of the people were making "desperate" attempts to avoid the net, but it was almost impossible to do so. Even if they succeeded in getting reclassified as the citizen of a homeland not yet "independent", they would be stripped of their South African citizenship whenever the local chiefs succumbed to Government pressure to take on the status of formal "independence." All particulars, including official tribal classification, homeland citizenship, personal records and fingerprints are stored in central computers and marked on the identity document:

"As a person cannot get work, get accommodation, marry, get a pension . . . or anything else without the identity document, few escape and those who do are likely to end up in prison where the particulars will be taken and sent to the computer anyway."

Once assigned to an "independent" bantustan, complete with Transkei or BophuthaTswana "passport", there is no escape:

"In law it does not matter what action they take. They are foreigners. Non-cooperation merely lays them open to the risks of deportation to a strange land as 'prohibited immigrants' or undesirable aliens."[17]

The Africans involved, as well as those who would find themselves in the same position if another bantustan accepted "independence", have lost their South African citizenship; but that does not mean that they will be treated in a consistent fashion as foreign visitors. The entire structure of discriminatory laws continues to apply; for these purposes, their foreign "passports" are treated as the old pass-books. The Government's Chief Bantu Commissioner for the Cape Province has been quoted as saying that Trasnskeian independence meant nothing to him, that Transkeians were still Africans and remained subject to the pass laws and other discriminatory legislation.[18] The Chief Commissioner for the Witwatersrand, the main industrial area, sought to reassure white employers concerned at the ill-defined status of their "Transkeian" and "Tswana" workers with an official circular in January 1979 saying that the Department of Plural Relations "does not see such people in the same light as it sees foreigners from, say, Malawi or Mozambique." The bantustan "passport" served exactly the same purpose as conventional pass books, for identification, and endorsements can be recorded in the passports.[19] This is quite incompatible with standard international practice concerning the passports of foreign nationals. Certainly no genuine foreigner in South Africa would expect to have his or her passport tampered with in this way. An early suggestion that Transkeians would be given the same status as white foreigners (or black visitors classified as "honorary whites") was strenuously denied by the Minister of Bantu Affairs in 1977; the Minister of Community Development said that there would be no difference between the position of Transkeians and the people of Soweto, Johannesburg's giant African township.[20]

Opposition to the bantustans

The organised opposition to the government's bantustan policies is either banned, imprisoned or in exile. The African National Congress (ANC) and the

Pan-Africanist Congress (PAC) were both banned in 1960, and in the succeeding years the liberation movement's leadership was arrested or forced to leave the country. In the years before 1960 the ANC, the oldest liberation movement in South Africa, played a leading role in many of the campaigns against the installation of the Bantu tribal authorities system, and both the ANC and PAC have consistently opposed the bantustan policy.

Reaction from urban Africans

Mrs. Sheena Duncan, in outlining the deprivation of South African citizenship which goes with bantustan "independence", warned that: "White South Africans should take note of the terrible anger this is causing in these children (being issued with passports at 16 instead of the expected reference books) and their parents."[21] After the experience of Transkei "independence", that of BophuthaTswana was received with a chorus of opposition from people in the urban areas who were classified as "Tswana". Letters to the African paper, *The World*, reflected these anxieties:

"I and hundreds of others are concerned that Chief Mangope has not had the guts to test our opinion by putting the independence issue to a referendum."[22]

"The Cabinet accept this empty echo because they are not going to suffer like us."[23]

"Many urban BophuthaTswana are going to lose their jobs like the Xhosa and be sent back to their poor, unfertile homeland."[24]

Black Consciousness organisations sent an open letter to Chief Mangope in July 1977 appealing to him "not to sell the souls of his people" by accepting a fraudulent independence. They added, "You and people like you are being used as pawns in the White man's intention of continuing the status quo . . . You are inherently part of South Africa."[25]

This kind of hostility towards bantustan chiefs on the part of urban Africans, who accuse them of selling out the blacks, has been observed on a number of formal occasions which bantustan "leaders" have tried to exploit for their own prestige. In 1974, a Black Renaissance Convention with delegates from all the black communities and organisations in South Africa condemned the bantustan policy and expelled anybody present who worked with it in any way — including Mr. Collins Ramusi, then a Minister of the Lebowa bantustan and perhaps the most radical of those involved.[26] In 1977, black urban leaders condemned bantustan chiefs for agreeing to new pass regulations without consulting urban Africans; they objected that the chiefs had no right to speak on their behalf. One of them, Mr. Baldwin Mudau, said: "The homeland leaders have committed a political blunder that will seal them off from future connections with urban people."[27]

At the mass funeral of Steve Biko, speakers called on blacks to reject bantustans entirely, and attacked the chiefs as "stooges, puppets and sell-outs."[28] Chief Buthelezi of KwaZulu, who often claims to be an urban as well as a bantustan leader, was expelled from the funeral service for Robert Sobukwe, head of the

Pan-African Congress, as were other bantustan personalities. An eye-witness of the event, Peter Brown, reported:

"My own view is that he (Buthelezi) was lucky to get out of there alive. One stumble, one better-directed stone, and anything might have happened . . . The hostility which forced Sonny Leon and the Transkei representatives and any other black person who had worked 'within the system' to leave was not as intense, but still very strong. They had to leave . . ."[29]

This intense hostility is all the more significant since it was directed at black collaborators only; sympathetic whites, of whom Peter Brown was one, were not asked to leave.

Various attempts to assess urban African opinion about the bantustans have indicated that the hostility shown on these occasions reflects the majority view. A survey of Soweto residents published in 1974 showed that two-thirds of the people refused to accept as their "real" home the bantustan to which they had been assigned. Three-quarters of them named Soweto as their real home. The survey concluded that there was "nearly universal" opposition to the bantustan concept, and that "the expressed attitudes are certainly not in line with official thinking."[30] Professor D. A. Kotze, in a lengthy study of African politics, stated that urban Africans are extremely sceptical about the bantustan idea, and only a tiny fraction of those eligible to be Transkei or Tswana voters registered or turned out for the elections. He explained:

"The low percentages in urban areas can partly be ascribed to the voters' fear that they would be endorsed out of the urban area if they identified too closely with a homeland."[31]

Faced with this kind of resistance, various forms of coercion are being tried by the South African authorities to direct urban Africans into the bantustan channels. The government has tried to make the right to a leasehold house in an urban area contingent on bantustan citizenship.[32] Mr. M. C. Botha, Minister of Bantu Administration, suggested that a whole range of preferences will be given to people who accept their bantustan identity.[33] Funds desperately needed for housing in the grossly overcrowded townships are being frozen by the East Rand Administration Board for example, and diverted to the construction of the Lebowa "capital", Lebowakgomo, which is intended to provide a base for long-distance commuters to the white areas.[34] Income from the urban townships in the Vaal Triangle, derived particularly from government sales of alcohol there, is being channelled into the bantustans instead of being used for township administration, arousing considerable opposition from the residents.[35] Pressures have been applied, where they can do so, by the bantustan chiefs to force urban Africans into line. Chief Maqoma, a member of the Ciskei Cabinet, warned those who were trying to avoid Ciskeian citizenship:

". . . those Ciskeians who do not obtain Ciskeian citizenship will find themselves in all sorts of difficulties."[36]

Relations between the bantustan chiefs and the urban majority of the African population, then, is one of intense confrontation. One of the leaders in Soweto,

Mr. Leonard Mosala, spoke for many others when he said, in response to the announcement of preferential treatment for bantustan citizens:

"This shows the eagerness of the nationalists to eliminate blacks in urban areas by force. But this will not be. Blacks are here to stay. No amount of pressure and intimidation will remove them. This will only cause frustration and insecurity and will harm race relations."[37]

CHAPTER 3

Independence?

By the end of 1979 three of the bantustans, Transkei,* BophuthaTswana and Venda were officially "independent". Although not recognised by any other country, these three are being presented by the South African Government as independent states with all the trappings of president, parliament, flag and even a diplomatic service, the crowning achievement and vindication of the bantustan policy and a model for the future development of the other territories.

The Transkei

In 1974 the Transkei was set on the path to "independence" with Chief Kaiser Matanzima's announcement under South African Government pressure that he had "changed his mind"; abandoning the position that independence was unthinkable unless the bantustan was given more land, he said it would now take place within five years.[1] The South African Government's commitment to this plan was made, curiously, not to Transkeians but to a meeting of white Nationalist Party members.[2] Less than a year later the Government had set the date (October 1976), reducing the transition from five years to two.

An attempt by Mr. Guzana, leader of the opposition party, to make independence contingent on a referendum of all Transkeians was defeated.[3] Chief Matanzima claimed that the elections of 1968 and 1973 had given his party, the TNIP, a mandate to call for independence — although in fact the TNIP had not received a majority of the vote, and their strength declined between the two elections.[4] Mr. Kobo, a spokesman of the opposition Democratic Party, said that the independence plan could result in economic disaster at a time of estimated unemployment of half a million people; he added that the Transkei could not "afford to rely on guarantees given by White South Africa, because promises have been made in the past and nearly all of them have been broken."[5] Another member of the Assembly, agreeing that independence was a suicidal move, added, "We want freedom, not independence."[6]

Strong criticism of Chief Matanzima's decision to request "independence" was also expressed by the other bantustan chiefs, on the grounds that he was breaking their united bargaining front arrived at in a summit meeting hosted by Chief Matanzima himself at Umtata. They had agreed that if any bantustan chiefs wanted to seek independence, they would decide on their course of action in consultation

---

*In recent years the South African Government has officially dropped the "the" before the Transkei and the Ciskei.

with the others; Chief Matanzima had failed to do this.[7] Matanzima claimed that independence would make no difference to people in the Transkei, or its nominal "citizens" outside:

"The only practical difference independence will make to the average Transkei citizens is that they will carry Transkei passports instead of Republican passes."[8]

It may be that the only difference he foresaw at the time was the promised payrise for himself and members of his entourage, as Prime Minister and members of the cabinet of a supposedly independent state.

The independence ceremonies, on 26 October 1976, took place in the face of total international boycott. Even the Rhodesian regime had failed to send a representative, and eight of the other nine bantustans ignored the occasion.[9] The London *Times* reported: "Transkei seems destined to remain a pariah among nations."[10] Most of the official opposition had been detained before the ceremony, as were two internationally known actors, John Kani and Winston Ntshona. A few days before independence, at least 10,000 Sotho-speaking people living in an area attached at the last minute to the Transkei, Glen Grey and Herschel districts, had fled in panic at the prospect of living under the Transkei establishment; leaders of the tiny QwaQwa bantustan, officially designated for Sothos, called for a national day of mourning on Transkei's independence day.[11]

When the Transkei became "independent", it launched a massive public relations campaign in favour of international recognition as a solution to its pariah · status. In this it was backed by all the resources of South Africa's Department of Information. An advertising campaign by the Department in international newspapers, promoting Transkei "independence", cost nearly R500,000 (£285,500). This seems to have been involved in the "Muldergate" scandal of irregular public relations deals; payment vouchers have not been produced for R100,000 of the total.[12] The advertising agency had been demanding cash in advance, on the grounds that many American papers would not accept political advertisements without advance payment.[13] In addition to this advertising, the Muldergate revelations have included free trips for many foreign journalists to the Transkei independence celebrations, and later to those of BophuthaTswana; in a secret memorandum, Dr. Eschel Rhoodie, then Secretary of the Department of Information, had said that money could be used to "buy" editorial space for articles "supplied by us or by journalists of the publication" as well as whole supplements on the Transkei financed by South African advertisements. Another technique would be "the 'buying' of the services of a journalist who then ostensibly supplies independent material for his publication while we pay him for his favourable opinion".[14]

Co-operation between the Department of Information and the Transkeian representatives over promoting the bantustan overseas was close. Mr. Digby Koyana, Transkei Minister of Justice, said that during his promotion tour of South Korea, Taiwan and Japan:

"Wherever we went, we had enough opportunity to preach the gospel of Transkei: to present the unanswerable case of Transkei's recognition. Of course, we had all the ammunition we needed, the various pamphlets of departments of Information and Tourism, and the independent reviews by Barclays' Bank and the *Daily Dispatch* which are all very convincing supplements to whatever one says by word of mouth."[15]

In pursuit of the elusive goal of international respectability, hundreds of thousands of Rands were spent directly from the Transkei's own budget on a handful of overseas agents, as reported by the *Rand Daily Mail* on the basis of a confidential memorandum from Mr. Koyana to Chief Matanzima. The agents included a Rhodesia-based travel agent Mr. Ishmail Khalpey, who received R32,000 (£18,000) for visits to India and Mauritius "to cultivate ground for a Ministerial visit"; Dr. Bruno Becchio, a lawyer operating in Switzerland, Holland and other parts of Europe, who received R90,000 (£51,000); Mr. Salim el-Hajj, a Lebanese working in the Middle East for the Transkei and collecting R225,000 (£128,000) for his services; Mr. Allan Phillips in Britain, with R21,000 (£12,000); and various unknown agents in the United States.[16]

Despite all this effort and expense, and considerable success in gaining a hearing for the Transkei in the world's press through favourable comment and advertisements, together with extensive foreign travel by representatives of the Transkei, the prospect of any country recognising it as an independent state seemed to become, if anything, even more remote. In a move clearly calculated to win some international credibility, in April 1978 the Transkei took the superficially drastic step of breaking "diplomatic relations" with South Africa. A month later, it announced its withdrawal from the "non-aggression pact" with South Africa.[17] The Transkeian Minister of Foreign Affairs told the world that "the announcement shook the bowels of the earth".[18] Others disagreed. Many people saw it as a rather desperate move by Matanzima to forestall massive defections from his own party; South African Government sources regarded it with equanimity as a gesture to international opinion that it was not a puppet of the South Africans.[19] Mr. Hans Abraham, a veteran Commissioner-General in the Transkei, dismissed Matanzima as "downright ungrateful" for all the help the South Africans had given him personally, and predicted that he would "come crawling back" if South Africa cut off his funds.[20] The announcement had remarkably little practical impact. A local observer, David Thomas, explained:

"It almost immediately became evident that the break was cosmetic. For appearances' sake ambassadors from each country were withdrawn and Transkei became more circumspect in its official dealings with South Africa. Money continued to pour in from South Africa and embassies and consulates were kept open with less senior staff under various pseudonyms like 'labour bureaux'."[21]

Both sides continued to enjoy diplomatic immunity.[22]

The South Africans also went ahead, unperturbed, with extensions and additions to its embassy in Umtata, the Transkei's capital.[23] The training of the 700-strong, largely ceremonial army was taken over for the time being by a group of Rhodesians, although the police continued to be trained by South Africa.[24]

As part of the effort to turn the "break" with South Africa to good advantage internationally, Chief Matanzima took on two British men, Mr. Humphrey

Berkeley and his colleague Mr. James Skinner, both of whom apparently believed in Transkei's "genuine independence".[25] Mr. Berkeley's job was to get recognition for Transkei, and Mr. Skinner's to promote its economic development as Managing Director of the Transkei Development Corporation. This latter proved to be even more difficult than the former. Mr. Skinner fired many of the white South Africans who were effectively running the Transkei economy and who, in his judgment, were not "capable, competent, and above all, loyal to Transkei."[26] Even more disturbing to the white South Africans was Mr. Skinner's apparent role in attempting to scrap racial segregation in Transkei schools and hospitals; the official organ of the National Party in the Cape, *Die Burger*, gave this front-page coverage, reporting whites in the Transkei to be outraged that their children would have to go to schools with black children; the Administrator of the Cape, Dr. L. Munnik, had "instituted an investigation".[27] The intense reaction from South Africa is understandable in terms of one of the guidelines in a Broederbond document of 1975 on separate development: "Certain measures are necessary for the maintenance of white identity (for example separate schools, living areas and the Immorality Act)."[28] It is quite consistent with this concern, and the overall interest of the Broederbond in the bantustans, that they should have secret cells among white South Africans in the Transkei. Head of the list exposed by journalists Ivor Wilkins and Hans Strydom was Mr. E. L. Brown, a former agent of South Africa's Bureau of State Security (BOSS) and then security adviser to Matanzima after independence. He was asked to leave after the information came out, but other alleged members remained, including a secretary in the Department of the Prime Minister who had drafted the Transkei Constitution. Dr. Hofmeyr, another Broeder, was expelled but only after refusing to admit a black child to his whites-only hospital in Umtata despite repeated requests.[29] The whites in the Transkei used the South African "embassy" as a meeting point, and it was used on at least one occasion for a National Party political meeting.[30]

The role of the Broederbond and of the South African Government in the subsequent treatment of Messrs. Skinner and Berkeley is unknown; however, they cannot have been sorry to see these two "trouble-makers" leave the Transkei, with its racial segregation intact. Skinner was dismissed first, and Berkeley — who was said to have been urging Matanzima to apply sanctions against Rhodesia and bring in Nigerian troops — was beaten up and "almost killed" by anonymous members of the Transkei security police. It is ironical that he survived by exploiting the ingrained fear of whites instilled into Africans in South Africa; after being beaten by them and lying in a pool of blood, Berkeley said, according to his own version of the incident, ". . . you are doing a wicked thing. I want you to kneel down and I'll say a prayer for you." Amazingly enough, they obeyed — then suddenly panicked and escaped in their car.[31] The assault coincided with a fierce attack on the same day by Chief Matanzima on "British jackals".[32] The attackers were never charged; shortly afterwards, Berkeley was officially dismissed. Skinner commented later that he and Berkeley had been "removed" from Transkei because they were an embarrassment to the efforts to restore diplomatic relations with South Africa.[33] An official delegation from the Transkei was then in Pretoria to discuss the topic with the new South African Prime Minister, P. W. Botha.[34]

BophuthaTswana

The Republic of South Africa consists of four provinces. The new "Republic of BophuthaTswana" consists of about eight pieces of territory, with undefined borders and in a state of continual change, spread over three of the provinces — Cape, Transvaal and the Orange Free State. The day of "independence" arrived with this bantustan in the process of being reduced from eight pieces to six; people were being bulldozed out of their farms in white areas, designated as "black spots", for removal to BophuthaTswana, while about 300,000 people living in the bantustan, but classified as non-Tswana, faced the prospect of expulsion from it.[35] The current borders of the bantustan were undefined in many areas; just before "independence", hundreds of the white farmers in the area were thoroughly confused as to which side of the border they were, and the Post Office, far from enlightening them, sent questionnaires to 300 of them to ask whether or not their farms were in BophuthaTswana. An official of the Vryburg Farmers' Union complained, "There has been confusion for the past ten years over the borders, and it's still the same today."[36]

To suit its convenience, South Africa has been changing the frontiers of BophuthaTswana at will, even after formal "independence". In order to resolve the problem of the South African "Embassy" being at Mafeking, just outside the borders of the bantustan but two kilometres from the new capital, Mmabatho, the boundary was moved a few hundred metres to accommodate the building, making that side of the street part of BophuthaTswana.[37] Otherwise, the borders are carefully drawn around towns and cities so that none of them, even if surrounded on three sides by the bantustan, actually belong to it; this applies to Pretoria, Rosslyn, Rustenburg and previously to Mafeking, although in September 1979 it was officially decided that Mafeking should join BophuthaTswana. The Johannesburg *Sunday Times* summed up the territory:

"There is no possible basis in morality or history to justify the arbitrary borders assigned to BophuthaTswana. They are merely the minimum that white greed could relinquish."[38]

The *Star* posed a particularly apt question to the puzzle of "the world's most separately-developed country":

"Could it be that the residents of these bits of land serve as a most useful labour reservoir for the industries of white South Africa?"[39]

It pointed out that 155,000 people cross the borders into South Africa every morning to work in these white towns and cities, including South Africa's capital, as "commuters".[40]

It is the comical nature of BophuthaTswana's territory that did most to detract from the independence ceremonies — an event which even the first independent bantustan, the Transkei, refused to recognise, on the grounds that a fragmented BophuthaTswana made the whole idea of independence ridiculous and so undermined Matanzima's own quest for international recognition. Transkei officials asserted that BophuthaTswana was truly a product of *apartheid*, which they claimed the Transkei was not. Further, the Transkei's diplomatic resources would be so strained by maintaining an embassy in BophuthaTswana that it would have no spare capacity if the moment came when they could establish a proper foreign mission somewhere. They therefore refused the BophuthaTswana initiative for establishment of diplomatic relations, some six months after the latter's independence.[41]

Independence was imposed on BophuthaTswana and on all Africans officially classified as Tswana, in the face of massive rejection of the idea. Hostility focused largely on the grim experiences of Africans allocated to the Transkei on its independence, particularly the repression of opposition and the treatment of urban Africans classified as Xhosa. The Black People's Convention (BPC) met, with ten other legal black organisations, at Hammanskraal a few months before the threatened independence of BophuthaTswana, and resolved to launch a campaign against bantustans and particularly this independence. They followed up with an "open-letter" — the first of its kind — to Chief Mangope, head of Bophutha-Tswana, appealing to him not to negotiate with the South Africans for independence. The letter challenged him to put the issue to the people involved in a referendum, otherwise:

". . . you and people like you, like Matanzima, are being used as pawns in the white man's intention of the continuation of the status quo in our country, by the use of power, and power only.

"You will be overtaken by the forces of justice and freedom, which has never been quenched in the hearts of the black people of South Africa."[42]

The South African Institute of Race Relations, a respectable body with a mainly white membership, issued an unusually strong statement on the issue calling on Mangope and the South African Government to "halt all plans for the independence of BophuthaTswana until such time as the future direction of the whole country can be decided by truly democratic processes."[43] At about the same time, the South African Council of Churches attacked the BophuthaTswana move and said that independence would deprive residents of bantustans of their "basic rights to share in the political, economic and social ordering of life in this country . . ."[44]

This broad opposition had no effect on the independence plans. Nor did the extremely low turn-out for elections immediately beforehand; only about 375,000 of the more than one million eligible to vote bothered to register,[45] and of these only half turned out to vote.[46] The most direct form of opposition was violence: the proposed BophuthaTswana Legislative Assembly in Mafeking was burnt to the ground in mass demonstrations a year before independence, and Mangope's own son was among those arrested. Later, Mangope and four of his Ministers were attacked when they tried to address an election meeting in an urban area.[47] The response to the constant threats of assassination and other violent incidents has been a clamp-down on opposition; Mangope told parents of the students active in the opposition that he felt the police should shoot indiscriminately in case of unrest, "in fact, I have told the police even to shoot my own child."[48] Opposition is intense; as the BPC and others' "open letter" put it:

"South Africa belongs to all its inhabitants and no one has the right to balkanise it. Why have 'your' people burned down 'your' Legislative Assembly when you claim to represent their interests? Why is it necessary for you to flee from meetings in the face of hurling of stones which come from 'your' people? You are not in a position to be independent. You are inherently part of South Africa, a part of the family of the people of South Africa. History, foreseeable history, will judge you and will sentence you."[49]

Independence, when it came on 6 December 1977, seemed remote from all this conflict. The big day was celebrated in Mmabatho ("Mother of the people") an instant capital created in six months just outside Mafeking on the edge of the Kalahari Desert. Its main features at independence were a red and yellow "meccano-style" Parliament building, a mansion for Mangope complete with bullet-proof windows and steel-lined walls, a luxury hotel with casino, a garage offering "farm fresh petrol", and a stadium made of scaffolding, all at various stages of construction.[50] A visiting journalist added that there was "nothing else. And when I say nothing else, I am not using a figure of speech. I mean, nothing else."

"This place, put down so carefully in the middle of nowhere, is one of the most bizarre I have ever seen. The capital of the Republic of BophuthaTswana! When one thinks of Soweto and its million or more inhabitants, living in those endless lines of identical little brick and asbestos houses . . . What makes it even more bizarre is that all the people taking advantage of these wonderful facilities (at the hotel) are white . . ."[51]

There is no town centre with shops or commercial buildings; electricity, water, sewerage and general supplies come from Mafeking.[52] This small and dusty South African "dorp" (small town) dominates Mmabatho; an African doctor's wife working in BophuthaTswana described being stopped at roadblocks all around Mafeking: "White soldiers and police still treat blacks like dirt."[53] The local mayor was interviewed about independence: glancing at his pistol holster, he told the reporter, "Independence for BophuthaTswana can't make much difference to us."[54] The country around Mafeking has in fact had a history of tin-pot republics being declared; a century ago, the Republics of Stellaland (around the dorp of Stella) and Goshen were proclaimed; they quickly disappeared, unrecognised even by fellow Afrikaners.[55]

The Department of Information in South Africa spent considerable sums on the travel and accommodation of foreign visitors to the independence event.[56] Hopes were not high, however; an international public relations consultant who had been involved in promoting the previous year's independence in the Transkei was quoted as saying:

"We had enough trouble selling the idea to the world. And at least, with Transkei in, more or less, one unified chunk of land, there was some argument for independence. With BophuthaTswana scattered in little slices of land, it is just a commodity nobody will buy."[57]

The effort to sell went ahead regardless: on the day of the official opening of the BophuthaTswana "Parliament" Chief Mangope was absent — on another foreign tour to seek international recognition.[58]

The independence event itself, according to *The Times*, was reminiscent of Evelyn Waugh's *Scoop*, a magnificent farce. A presidential salute fired by South African field guns caused cows grazing in the fields round the parliament building to bolt in panic. The official in charge of press relations seemed to take delight in telling journalists that they would not be admitted to most of the functions and refused to release names of invited guests. The programme was almost identical to that developed for Transkei: a football match, dances and a gymnastic display — boycotted by all urban athletes. Just before midnight, flags were exchanged, the new BophuthaTswana National Guard presented arms, a South African band played various anthems, guns boomed and an independence flame was kindled.[59]

At a champagne reception to open the new Mmabatho Sun casino, there was consternation when a South African official's wife turned up in a dress almost identical to those worn by the African girls in the BophuthaTswana choir. The Mayoress of Mafeking, resplendent in a full-length pink crimplene and chiffon gown, showed off her knowledge of the natives:

"The main thing is that we still have to have servants, especially uncultured servants, and we still have to be responsible for them. You get your smart ones, but those not getting schooling we are still responsible for — otherwise they pinch and steal."[60]

South Africa's Deputy Commissioner of Police was a prominent guest at the celebrations.[61]

The meaning of all these events was, at best, confused. Many school pupils and teachers boycotted all the events, and some people found it revolting that a feast should be prepared in their midst while they were mourning the death in detention of Steve Biko.[62] Urban Tswana-speaking people complained that they had not been informed about independence or its consequences, let alone consulted, although they were being forced to become citizens of the newly independent bantustan.[63] Chief Mangope produced a series of excuses and complaints about South Africa's handling of the affair and its blithe ignoring of his demands for more land and the inclusion of some proper towns. He said at one stage that during the independence negotiations he had thought he had won a concession from the South Africans over citizenship, realising only later that this was not so.[64] In his independence address he described the fragments of territory making up his new entity as a "territorial credibility gap". "Just as it is born, our independence has already fallen into a fatal credibility gap — the territorial credibility gap, which bears the stamp 'Made in Pretoria'." Mr. M. C. Botha, who had conducted the negotiations on the South African side, said later that in the case of BophuthaTswana as well as of the Transkei, they had been long-winded and boring — apparently they had been a mere formality as far as the South Africans were concerned. Botha said his patience had sometimes been "sorely tried" by the attempts of the black delegations to get a better deal, although after each meeting press statements had been issued saying that discussions had taken place in a cordial atmosphere.[65] Further contradictions were evident on Mangope's side; he accepted a form of independence in December that he had angrily denounced the previous July as the South African Government "trying to trick us into an independence with smells of fraud and disgrace . . . an independence which will only cater for certain white people's evil dreams of continued baaskap (domination), privilege and discrimination . . ."[66]

In some respects, BophuthaTswana's independence remained at the level of rhetoric. Thousands of white as well as black South Africans, who in theory needed passports and permits, found themselves crossing in and out of parts of the bantustan on a regular basis — without knowing or caring. There were no signs or border posts on most roads, and no fences or other markings.[67] An attempt to achieve status and incidentally some revenue, through the issue of Bophutha-Tswana postage stamps, rather backfired; the message, "Overeating is dangerous" together with knife, fork and spoon with the sign of a skull, was greeted with horror in the international press in the light of the terrible poverty and malnutrition in the bantustan, resulting in a high percentage of deaths from starvation.[68] Equally unsuccessful was a major attempt to put BophuthaTswana on the map by backing, at enormous expense, a world championship boxing tournament at the Mmabatho Sun. Attendance was very poor, and most of the R500,000 spent on the gamble by BophuthaTswana was lost.[69]

The most enduring monument to BophuthaTswana grandeur remains the Mmabatho hotel and casino, built by a South African hotel chain to take advantage of the loophole allowing gambling so close to the white population centres around Pretoria, Johannesburg and the Rand. The nucleus of a planned R30-million Southern Sun entertainment and sports complex, the casino is to sport an artificial lake with a wave-making machine for surfing, and a grandiose golf course which is the pet scheme of Gary Player.[70] He will be resident professional and golf director, and boasts: "For the first time in Southern Africa we will see a golf course that is correctly built." This will mean elaborate drainage, mounding and modern tee and grass shapes, as well as spectacular vantage points built for spectators and television cameras.[71] To complete the entertainment, 40,000 hectares of Bophutha-Tswana will be made into a game reserve.[72]

While not officially segregated, the complex is available only to those with the necessary cash — and that excludes virtually all Africans, making it in effect a pleasure-ground for whites. A visiting journalist reported that a year after independence the gambling room, containing "battery upon battery of one-armed bandits", was crammed with white South Africans, earnestly pulling the levers. There was a single African playing during his visit, performing for an admiring group of locals too poor to play themselves.[73] Among the machines is a "special" that pays out the biggest jackpot in Africa, R5,000 (£2,855) a time for those who can afford to play it.[74]

The lone African playing the whites' gambling machines was probably one of the tiny elite created by South Africa's bantustan policy, and particularly the process of independence which offers big pay rises all round for those Africans prepared to go along with the deal despite their people's opposition. The salaries are astronomical in comparison with African wage-levels generally: Chief Mangope, for example, started on R26,280 a year (£15,000), part of it tax-free, on independence day, while Cabinet Ministers earn R18,040 (£10,300), their deputies R15,680 (£8,950), and ordinary members of the National Assembly R4,800 (£2,740).[75] There are luxury extras on top of the salaries: Mangope, for example, acquired a bullet-proof, luxury Mercedes limousine specially made for him in West Germany for R47,000 (£26,800). It was described as having so much armour-plating that "it would make a tortoise feel naked in comparison".[76] Housing is another extra, and luxury homes are under construction at Mmabatho, conveniently close to the casino, for the white officials seconded from the South African Government, and for the Ministers of the BophuthaTswana Government.[77] A cousin of Chief Mangope, posted as "consul" to nearby Bloemfontein, was bought a luxury suburban house for R72,000 (£41,000) The white residents seemed tolerant of the idea of a single African family in their midst — their own servants, after all, live in their own back yards — and envious of the grossly inflated price agreed to by the BophuthaTswana Government for this purpose, almost double the actual value.[78] All this lavish spending was not lost on African observers; *The Voice*, for example, commented bitterly that "BophuthaTswana derives the bulk of its capital income from the sale of labour in the Republic of South Africa where about two thirds of the Batswana people live."[79]

Meanwhile, people living in BophuthaTswana are hungry and unemployed. The *Rand Daily Mail* has reported this as the reason behind "a wave of lawlessness of an intensity never experienced before in Tswana villages." At the time of independence, hungry people raked through rubbish bins at the Mmabatho Sun hotel.[80] The transition had an immediate and disastrous impact on some; for example, many Africans who were receiving small pensions as veterans of the Second World War were reclassified as BophuthaTswana citizens, and had their pensions cut off by South Africa.[81] Over two million people classified as Tswana found their South African citizenship removed overnight. Most serious of all, the 300,000 people living inside BophuthaTswana but not classified as Tswanas suddenly found themselves under pressure from Mangope to take up BophuthaTswana citizenship, under the threat of deportation from their homes to unknown destinations if they refused. Non-Tswana traders (79% of all the African traders in the bantustan) were also threatened with deportation if they refused to take out citizenship.[82] After a series of violent incidents and the suppression by the South African police of general resistance to the change — centered on the enormous sprawling "squatter" settlements around the big industrial and employment centres, particularly at Winterveldt — people were forced to abandon their protests in order to keep their homes, and started to apply for citizenship. More than 250,000 people classified as Ndebele, living north of Pretoria, abandoned their refusal to take out citizenship only after being intimidated by threats from Mangope personally that he would stop payment of teachers' salaries, close the schools, harrass Ndebeles in the Babalegi industrial area of BophuthaTswana and stop the payment of pensions to old people, unless they dropped their opposition.[83]

The deportations and associated violence around Winterveldt are among the worst examples of South African removals, complicated by the issue of Bophutha-Tswana citizenship, loss of South African citizenship and the involvement of the BophuthaTswana Government in the forefront of the official attack on the squatters. The events at Winterveldt are described in more detail in Chapter 6.

Venda

The Venda bantustan became "independent" on 13 September 1979. A month earlier a group of journalists was taken on a tour of the territory, where they saw evidence of massive and rapid construction work, including a parliament building costing R5 million, a training school for police, army and prison officers, a large stadium for the independence celebrations and residences for cabinet ministers and civil servants. The Venda capital is Sibasa/Thohoyandou, the territory's only size-able town.

Venda's independence took place despite the fact that the ruling party lost the 1978 election to the opposition, retaining power only through the nominated members and South African support. On 30 August the Chief Minister Patrick Mphephu was installed as Paramount Chief of Venda by the South African Minister of Manpower Utilisation in a move designed to consolidate Mphephu's tribal and political dominance.

Thousands of residents were accomodated in tents for the independence cere-monies which culminated in a 100-gun salute as State President Viljoen conferred Venda's new status at a midnight ceremony. The following morning the stadium was found to be strewn with pamphlets issued by the ANC denouncing the bantu-stan.[84]

Who's next?

Independence is not an option for the bantustans; it is the logical extension of the whole policy. An attempt in 1977-78 to provide for an alternative to indepen-dence, called "autonomy", and which had been welcomed with enthusiasm by bantustan politicians as a way out of Transkei, BophuthaTswana and Venda patterns, was quietly scrapped by the South African Government in the middle of the parliamentary proceedings. It had been recognised, reportedly, as a "major blunder" running counter to National Party (and Broederbond) policy. The major difference would have been that people assigned to an "autonomous" bantustan would not have been deprived of their South African citizenship. It was realized that if "autonomy" became a feasible possibility, the Government would probably never be able to persuade other bantustan leaders to face the opposition of their nominal subjects by accepting independence. Moreover, the chiefs of the Transkei and BophuthaTswana had proved extremely resentful at the prospect of other bantustans having the option of autonomy which had not been available to them.[85]

Bantustan politicians are somewhat wary of accepting independence — an irrevocable step and one which is not conducive to good relations with the people. Following a meeting of all except the Transkei chiefs in 1976, they issued a joint statement to the effect that with the exception of BophuthaTswana, the chiefs wished to "reiterate that they have no intention whatever of opting for so-called independence, as we do not want to abdicate our birthright as South Africans as well as forfeiting our share of the economy and wealth which we have jointly built."[86]

This was by no means the end of the argument, however. Three months later, Mr. A. J. Raubenheimer, Minister of Water Affairs, told a National Party meeting that the South African Government would cut off financial help to those bantustans which did not ask for independence. He added:

"If they don't want it we can't force them, but if they don't want it we can't be bothered."

Since about 80% of the bantustans' budgets are supplied direct from Pretoria, the threat was a serious one. Chief Buthelezi of the KwaZulu bantustan complained bitterly, "In one breath he says his Government will not force the homelands to accept independence and in the next he says it will starve them into acceptance."[87] The following year, KwaZulu had R4 million (£2.3 million) cut unexpectedly from its South African subsidy for the year, which Buthelezi linked with Raubenheimer's statement. He said that the reduced budget would mean fewer people getting pensions, fewer teachers, no money for the free school-books planned and the abandonment of certain agricultural schemes.[88]

In the face of this financial pressure, the Ciskei bantustan is being prepared for independence despite the earlier opposition, and others may follow soon. The chiefs of Venda and Ciskei were the only ones from any bantustans to attend the rather lonely BophuthaTswana celebrations.[89] When Venda gained "independence" the South Africans made little or no attempt to "sell" the idea as they had with the Transkei and BophuthaTswana. As each bantustan is readied for independence, there is a growing credibility gap already illustrated by the Transkei's contemptuous dismissal of the BophuthaTswana claims: each "independence" is more improbable than the last. In particular, the device used by the South Africans to add territory to the Transkei and BophuthaTswana as a kind of independence dowry — removing it from other bantustans, respectively Ciskei and QwaQwa — leaves the others rather threadbare. Dr. P. S. Hattingh, a research officer at the Africa Institute, has pointed out that the Transkei and BophuthaTswana between them absorbed more than half the total amount of land set aside for African reserves under the 1936 and 1913 legislation, or about 7% of the total land area of the Republic of South Africa.[90] Since, as indicated in Chapter 1, only about 11.9% of the country has in fact been turned over to the bantustans, this leaves an actual amount of available land — given the minimal budget now available for land purchase — of only 4.8% of the total, to be shared according to the official plans between the eight remaining bantustans yet to become "independent" states. How

South Africa will deal with the diminishing returns of its drive for bantustan independence remains to be seen.

The bid for international recognition of South Africa's separate development policy, in the shape of independent bantustans, has been unsuccessful despite the money and public relations expertise devoted to the project; further independence celebrations are likely to hinder that process rather than help it. The numbers of scattered fragments of reserve land, their constantly shifting character, the inadequacy of the total land allocated, the extension of bantustan citizenship to millions of urban Africans against their will, the lack of economic viability — none of these factors can quite be covered up by the insistent focus on the trappings of independence such as highly-paid Prime Ministers and Presidents, flags, anthems, stadiums, lavish ceremonies and the rest. The independent bantustans are a creation of the South African Government, in the teeth of the most vigorous opposition by virtually all Africans except the highly-paid chiefs who stand to benefit personally. As the statement of the BPC-led meeting cited above argued, a nation is a historically evolved and stable entity, a community of people with a common territory and economic life.[91] Accepting the bantustans would mean the African and other black people of South Africa abandoning their birthright, the whole country of South Africa whose vast wealth "is due mainly to the exploitation of black people who have the right of and hope for sharing the product of the labour eventually."[92]

Similarly the South African liberation movements, the ANC and the PAC, have always clearly stated that the bantustan scheme has no place in their vision of a future South Africa.

ANC President O. R. Tambo said in his statement to the United Nations on 26 October 1976:

"We state now, as we stated then (at the inception of the bantustan programme), that an incontrovertible part of the demands of our people is that there shall be one united and democratic South Africa. We will never abandon our birthright to the ownership and control of the whole territory of our country nor countenance any attempt to Balkanise it, and to set its people one against another in tribal, racial or national conflicts."[93]

CHAPTER 4

Outlines of the Bantustans

Area and population

The exact extent of the African reserve areas has been a matter of dispute ever since they were created. Statistics provided in January 1972 by the official magazine *Bantu*, for instance, are inconsistent with those issued in 1971 by the Department of Statistics.[1] In 1974 the Department of Bantu Affairs and Development, in collaboration with the various Deeds Offices, was still in the process of checking the extent of land held by the South African Bantu Trust, an agency of the government, as well as by individual Africans.[2] Mr. M. C. Botha, former Minister of Bantu Administration, said at the time the examination of records began that no exact statistics were available; in addition, the extremely complicated categorisation of different kinds of reserve land might be amended, changing the final result.[3] A total figure with break-down according to the various different bantustans was finally produced at the end of 1976: 15,551,000 hectares.[4] The detailed breakdown is given in Table 1.

The population of the bantustans is also a matter of uncertainty, since the latest census figures for 1970 are generally thought to be unreliable. So many Africans are present in urban areas without authorisation that the urban population is seriously undercounted; and many of those in the bantustans would have their reasons, such as fear of taxation, to give distorted information. For what they are worth, the census figures indicate that of the 15 million Africans counted in South Africa, eight million were in "white areas" outside the bantustans, and seven million inside.[5] Official ideology has the entire African population allocated to one or other of the bantustans, despite the fact that the majority have never lived there (and probably a larger majority than the official figures indicate). The result is the rather bizarre situation where for most of the bantustans, and for the group as a whole, more than half the people allocated to them on paper have no connections there. In official terms, the *de facto* population is less than half the *de jure* population. Table 1 shows the situation for each of the bantustans in this regard.

The ten bantustans

The South African government classifies Africans according to its own categories of "tribe"; regardless of each individual's identification with one or more tribes, or with none, they are officially assigned to one or other of the ethnic groupings by white officials. The categories are the basis of the bantustan policy, with the general idea being a homeland for each tribe which is officially recognised

Table 1 — Area and population of the bantustans

Bantustan	"Tribe"	Area[1] (1,000 hectares)	Area after completion of consolidation[2] (1,000 ha.)	Number of pieces	Number of pieces after consolidation[3]	Total African population[4] (1,000)	Population of the "tribe" in the bantustan[5] (1,000)	De jure population[4] (1,000)	% of the de jure population in the bantustan*
Bophutha-Tswana	Tswana	3,800	4,043	7	6	1,154	600	2,103	29
Ciskei	Xhosa	533	770	18 (plus black spots)	1	475	510**	872	58
Gazunkulu	Shangaan (Tsonga)	675	741	4	3	333	234	814	29
KaNgwane	Swazi	370	391	3 (plus about 10 black spots)	1	209	82	590	14
KwaZulu	Zulu	3,100	3,239	44 (plus 144 black spots)	10	2,691	2,057	5,029	41

Bantustan	"Tribe"[1]	Area[1] (1,000 hectares)	Area after completion of consolidation[2] (1,000 ha.)	Number of pieces	Number of pieces after consolidation[3]	Total African population[4] (1,000)	Population of the "tribe" in the bantustan[5] (1,000)	De jure population[4] (1,000)	% of the de jure population in the bantustan[*]
Lebowa	N. Sotho (N. Ndebele and Pedi)	2,200	2,518	14	6	1,388	946	2,234	42
Ndebele	S. Ndebele	75	73	1	2	150	150	—	—
QwaQwa	S. Sotho (Shoeshoe)	48	62	1	1	91***	24	1,698	1
Transkei	Xhosa	4,100	4,501	3	3	2,391	1,651	4,250	39
Venda	Venda	650	668	3 (plus 1 black spot)	2	339	239	449	53

* This is an approximation only, since the figures refer to different years and are affected by population growth, migration, removals, consolidation and the transfer of land from one bantustan to another.

** This was before the transfer of a large section to Transkei.

*** The population in 1978 was reported to have reached over 200,000. (*The Star*, Johannesburg, 2.12.78.)

Sources
1. *Debates*, 7 (1977), cols. 596–7.
2. Bureau for Economic Research re Bantu Development (Benbo), *Black Development in South Africa* (Johannesburg, 1976). p. 23, Table 3. 4.
3. *Debates*, 17 (1977), col. 1196.
4. Projections for 1976, based on 1970 census figures, by Benbo; quoted in South African Institute of Race Relations, *A Survey of Race Relations, 1977* (Johannesburg, SAIRR, 1978.) p. 311.
5. Muriel Horrell, *The African Homelands of South Africa* (SAIRR, 1973). Later figures are not available.

by the government. There are some serious anomalies, however, even according to this simplistic division: for one of the official tribes, the Xhosas, there are two bantustans (the Transkei and Ciskei); one bantustan, Lebowa, is officially for two different tribes; while for many there is none at all.

The tribal classifications are loosely based on the whites' anthropological findings, an old-fashioned and frankly racist approach to a different society which uses differences in language and dialect, geography, or other criteria to distinguish between "tribes" of Africans, but not of Europeans. The official approach completely rejects any suggestion that Afrikaners and English are separate tribes, for example, let alone German, Portuguese, Jewish or Greek South Africans. In the case of the African population there are basically only two distinct linguistic groupings, Nguni and Sotho, and these are closely related to each other. South Africa being a highly urbanised country for all racial groups, any correlation between official classification by tribe and the reality of separation into different areas and language groups which may once have existed has been seriously eroded. In fact one could go further than this. ANC leader Govan Mbeki said in his book *Transkei: The Peasants Revolt*, which was published abroad just as he and other ANC leaders were sentenced to life imprisonment in 1964:

"of the total African population of South Africa less than one third lives in, or comes from the 'homelands'. The great majority live, were born, and work either in the cities or on the farms of 'white' South Africa. South Africa is a single multi-national society, integrated and inter-dependent. This is the reality which the apostles of apartheid seek to disclaim."[6]

Where a large group of Africans not officially recognised claim classification as a "tribe" and allocation to a new bantustan, they are likely to be rudely rejected by government officials. A recent case of this was the AmaHlubi group with 1.5 million adherents scattered (like most of the others) all over South Africa, but categorised against their will as Zulus. A similar claim was made at about the same time by a leader of the Molife people, also in KwaZulu. The response to these kinds of claims, often based on a group's history as an entity distinct from those they are officially categorised with, tends to be brusque. A representative of the Department of Plural Affairs in Pretoria said of the Molife claim:

"The Government would never dream of giving any petty little chief like this independence. We do not have a tribal policy. We have a national policy. For example it would be wrong to say KwaZulu is the homeland for the Zulu tribe. There are 301 or 302 tribes in KwaZulu which together made up the Zulu nation. The Government would not be interested in giving each tribe independence."[7]

This is a most interesting admission that the entities officially used to categorise Africans are not actually tribes, but arbitrary groups of tribes whose identity is considered irrelevant; they are glorified by the term "nation" although they have never been nations.

There are ten bantustans, and even in terms of the official "national" categorisation the distribution of people among them is somewhat irrational. In some areas

Table 2 — **Official tribal allocations for each bantustan**

Bantustan	"Nation"	% of "nation" in the bantustan*	Population of "nation" in other bantustans (1,000)	% of "nation" in other bantustans	Population of other "nations" in the bantustan (1,000)	% of other "nations" in the bantustan**
Bophutha-Tswana	Tswana	29	10	1.7	284	25
Ciskei***	Xhosa***	58	46	2.1	14	3
Gazunkulu	Shangaan (Tsonga)	29	159	40.4	33	10
KaNgwane	Swazi	14	30	26.9	36	17
KwaZulu	Zulu	41	77	3.6	39	1
Lebowa	N. Sotho (N. Ndebele and Pedi)	42	23 (N. Ndebele) 102 (Pedi)	33.1 10.2	138	10
Ndebele	S. Ndebele	—	55	100.0	0	0
QwaQwa	S. Sotho (Shoeshoe)	1	120	83.2	1	1
Transkei***	Xhosa***	39	46	2.1	83	3
Venda	Venda	53	12	4.7	25	7

* From the calculation in Table 1.

** Using total African population for each bantustan as at the end of 1976, given in Table 1.

*** These figures relate to all Xhosas in relation to both Transkei and Ciskei.

NB: All figures refer to the 1970 census apart from those taken from Table 1. All figures are approximations.

Sources

Muriel Horrell, *The African Homelands of South Africa* (South African Institute of Race Relations, Johannesburg, 1973).

Bantu, January 1972.

P. S. Hattingh, "Consolidation of Black Homelands", in *Bulletin of the Africa Institute*, Pretoria, No. 4, 1975.

the majority of the people are categorised as a group other than that for which the bantustan was intended. As Table 1 shows, the majority of each "nation" lives outside the bantustan concerned in almost all cases, either in some other bantustan or in the white area. Over 83% of the 1.7 million "South Sotho" live in other bantustans. Table 2 gives details of the distribution of each "nation" in the bantustans.

The legal basis

Legislation for the native reserves, later known as the "Bantu homelands", has been very closely linked with the removal of Africans' civil rights in South Africa as a whole. A number of the measures deal with both these elements together.

The idea of territorial segregation was recognized in legislation in 1913, with the *Natives Land Act*, which "scheduled" certain of the areas already in African occupation, and prohibited Africans from acquiring land in any other parts of the country.[8] The scheduled areas were never surveyed, and most of them have still not been.

The *Native Affairs Act*, No. 23 of 1920 provided for the extension of the Transkeian Territories General Council principle to other areas where the Africans so wished; in the event it was not widely adopted.[9] The *Native Administration Act*,* No. 38 of 1927, together with the South African constitution of 1909, gave the Governor-General (now the State President) the power to legislate for the Transkei without prior reference to parliament, by simple proclamation.[10] Shortly before this, in 1923, the system of influx control was established along the lines recommended by the Stallard Commission, in the *Natives (Urban Areas) Act*, (consolidated later as Act No. 25 of 1945). The structure of the present bantustans was therefore laid in the 1920s, with the establishment of Presidential power over the reserves, and the reversion to migrant labour.

A major factor was the *Representation of Natives Act*, which finally removed Africans from the common voting roll of the Cape Province (an "entrenched clause" in the Constitution), thus completing the process which had begun in 1910 when Africans were excluded from membership of parliament. The Natives' Representative Council, a body with no statutory powers, was established as compensation, together with the "release" of certain areas for possible future purchase by the South African Native Trust, or by African tribes and individuals. Not all the "released areas" have yet been bought.

With the coming into power of the Nationalist party, a series of specific measures were undertaken which enshrined the principle of territorial separation as such. The first was the *Bantu Authorities Act*, No. 68 of 1951, establishing local "tribal authorities"; this measure, together with the *Bantu Education Act*, No. 47

---

*Now the Black Administration Act. This approach is reflected in all South Africa's racial legislation; originally they referred to Africans as "natives", then "Bantu", and more recently "black". When the term "Bantu" was officially dropped in 1979, all legislation and regulations using the term automatically replaced it with "black".

of 1953, and other measures, established the ground rules. An integral part of the 1951 Act was the abolition of the Natives' Representative Council, set up by the 1936 Act as compensation for the loss of the franchise. Dr. Verwoerd, in the debate on the Bill, made no pretence that Africans agreed to these steps:

"These proposals were not very warmly welcomed by the Bantu leaders, for they had but one desire—they repeatedly said so—and that was equality and representation in the Union Parliament together with the Europeans. They very expressly said that this was their sole aim in their constitutional development . . ."[11]

The *Promotion of Bantu Self-Government Act*, No. 46 of 1959, according to the government publication *Bantu*, "gave the Bantu peoples of South Africa a categoric assurance that the South African government had irrevocably set a course on a road that would lead the homelands to meaningful self-government."[12] It established a number of white Commissioners-General to act as agents of the Central Government in the homelands, and set up the eight Bantu authorities. It also completed the process of removing Africans' civil rights, with the elimination of the (white) Native Representatives from the House of Assembly and Senate.

In 1968 came the *Promotion of the Economic Development of Bantu Homelands Act*, No. 46 of 1968. This was concerned mainly with the consolidation of previous legislation governing the financing of development in African areas, and the functions of the Bantu Investment Corporation (BIC), Xhosa Development Corporation (XDC) and any future bodies to be set up along those lines. In debate, it was made clear that no links with any kind of "alien interests" would be tolerated.[13]

The *Bantu Homelands Citizenship Act*, No. 26 of 1970, provides for all "Bantu" in South Africa to be given citizenship of one of the "Homelands", and for each to be issued with a certificate of this citizenship. There was considerable fear among urban Africans that this measure would be used to strip them of their few remaining rights under Section 10 of the 1945 Urban Areas Act, and to force them into the "migratory" labour pattern. The Minister of Bantu Administration and Development confirmed their fears during the debate on the Act when, speaking of the Section 10 rights, he announced:

"I am going to remove all and every one of them."[14]

The *Bantu Homelands Constitution Act*, No. 21 of 1971, provides for the South African State President to issue a proclamation establishing legislative assemblies, without the necessity of consulting the South African House of Assembly. He can also proclaim any of the bantustans a self-governing Territory, giving it the theoretical right, subject to the South African President's veto, to legislate for any of its "citizens" whether inside or outside the bantustan itself.[15] It also provides for Bantu Affairs Administration Boards (composed of whites) to supervise the affairs of Africans living in white areas.

The *Constitution Amendment Act*, No. 1 of 1971, was intended to complement the Bantu Homelands Constitution Act by giving the State President the power to determine as an official language one or more African languages in each of the homelands. This is remarkable chiefly for the fact that it removes the last remaining "entrenched clause" in the South African Constitution. It also transfers to the State President power which should be exercised by parliament.

In the case of Namibia (South-West Africa), the *Development of Self-Government for Native Nations in South-West Africa Act*, No. 54 of 1968, provides for Bantu Authorities in the bantustans being established in Namibia, as in the 1951 *Bantu Authorities Act*, No. 68 of 1951, and the *Promotion of Bantu Self-Government Act*, No. 46 of 1959. This is part of the implementation of the Odendaal Commission's Report, which recommended the virtual annexation and partition of Namibia, formerly an internationally mandated territory. The Odendaal Report was held up while the International Court of Justice was considering the contentious case against South Africa, but at the refusal to adjudicate in 1966, the plan was immediately put into operation.

The *Bantu Laws Amendment Act*, No. 7 of 1973, was designed to speed up planning for the partial consolidation contained in the Bantu Administration Act of 1927, whereby although the government could order any African or group of Africans to move from one place to another, the order could not be enforced in the face of refusal to move until a resolution to that effect had been adopted by both Houses of Parliament. The 1973 Act provided for the approval by Parliament of broad plans, which could then be implemented as required by the government; no groups or individuals then had any way to resist an enforced move. The Act stipulated that before issuing a deportation or removal order, the Minister of Bantu Administration and Development must consult with the bantustan government concerned. During the debate on this, the Deputy Minister stated that consultation did not necessarily mean that the order should be agreed upon. A further provision of the Act was to enable the South African government to reserve for African occupation land in an urban area which is surrounded by or adjoining a bantustan.[16] This has been used for the creation of "bantustan" townships which may be completely removed from any other bantustan area, and serve merely as the dormitory area for African workers in a "white" urban centre.

The *Bantu Laws Amendment Act*, No. 70 of 1974, provided for the delegation of existing powers over the bantustans to lower authorities within the South African government. Since power is vested in the State President, often overriding the normal power of the Parliament to review legislative changes in the case of the bantustans, this provides the Minister of Bantu Development and even comparatively minor officials with absolute power in many areas over the nominal chiefs who form the "governments" of the bantustans, at a time when they are supposedly gaining greater autonomy and responsibility for their own affairs.[17]

Also in 1974 the *Second Bantu Laws Amendment Act*, No. 71 of 1974, enabled bantustan "governments" to prohibit any organisation with African members, and to stop the furtherance of the objects of such organisations, within the bantustans. They could further restrict to a remote area any organisation or individual, and prohibit the "publication or dissemination of the contents of any speech, utterance, writing or statement of any Bantu." These powers are available for the South African government to apply throughout the Republic; however, the fact that banning of individuals, organisations and publications is the first police power to be assigned to the bantustan chiefs in their own right is significant of the overall trend of the chiefs towards entrenching their own position by means of outlawing any opposition (see further Chapter 6). At no point, however, can the chiefs use their own discretion; the Act states that if and when any bantustan government equips itself with the repressive powers concerned, they must be exercised with the prior approval of the Minister of Bantu Administration and Development.[18]

The most recent spate of legislation has concerned measures to make the bantustans "independent"; starting with the *Status of the Transkei Act,* No. 100 of 1976, there has been an elaborate series of changes made to give effect to Transkei, BophuthaTswana and other bantustans' removal of the "citizens" assigned to them from any official existence in the Republic of South Africa.

Legislation on the bantustans is complex; however, the actual legal position on the ground is one of almost total confusion as to who has final responsibility for any particular service or regulation; major points of law remain impossible to define. Overall, the effect of this body of law is to institutionalise racial segregation in minute detail. In the words of Professor John Dugard, international law expert at the University of Witwatersrand:

"Basically, the law fulfills four functions. First, it constructs a legal order based on racial discrimination and differentiation. Secondly ... by legitimizing discriminatory practices, it neutralizes the immorality of such practices in the eyes of the majority of the White population who accept without question any rule which has been blessed by Parliament. Thirdly, those laws which institutionalize separate development provide a convenient facade for the outside world. The Promotion of Bantu Self-Government Act, the Transkei Constitution and the Bantu Homelands Constitution Act are useful for foreign consumption as they adopt the rhetoric of self-determination and self-government without disclosing the realities of South African life. Legal tinsel is used to conceal the fact that most of the African population lives outside the homelands and cannot in fact participate in the homelands' political process; that the African people themselves have not been consulted about their future; and that self-determination inside or outside the homelands is meaningless while the harsh security laws remain in force. Fourthly, the drastic security laws ... create a repressive atmosphere in which meaningful political debate and activity is stifled."[19]

Security legislation

On "independence", bantustans have effectively adopted South African legislation on all security matters. An important precedent was the Transkei Public Security Act, which came into force in 1977. This makes it an offence equivalent to treason to refuse to recognise the Transkei's "independence" or advocate that it should be "part of another country" (i.e. South Africa), and prescribes a maximum sentence of death. The major provisions of South African security legislation, including indefinite detention without trial, are incorporated in the Public Security Act. In terms of the Act all security laws applicable in South Africa were repealed (including the Suppression of Communism Act, the Internal Security Act, the Riotous Assemblies Act, the Unlawful Organisations Act, and also the Transkei Emergency Laws contained in Proclamation R400). Many of the measures provided for in these Acts, however, are incorporated in the new legislation.

The major terms of this Act are:

1. Anyone propagating or disseminating views that Transkei, or other parts of Transkei, should form another country or part of another country, will be guilty of a treasonable offence, and liable to the death sentence.

2. It is an offence to harbour or help terrorists, the maximum penalty being death.

3. It is an offence to make statements or commit acts causing hostility between population groups.

4. It is an offence to belong to certain organisations declared unlawful by the State President.

5. The State President may authorise a chief to banish any person to another area, either permanently or for a specified period.

6. The State President may order a tribe or part of a tribe to be removed, without warning, to another area if he considers it to be in the public interest.

7. The Minister of Justice may ban gatherings of more than ten people, prevent individuals from attending certain gatherings and declare a State of Emergency if he deems it necessary.

8. Provision is made for the banning of persons, for detention without trial, and for the arrest, without warrant, of any person for interrogation purposes, after which arrest there may be no recourse to the courts to obtain the release of such person.[20]

In 1979 the South African government gave all the bantustans powers to ban and banish people under the Black States Constitution Act of 1979.

CHAPTER 5

Inside the Bantustans

One of the main effects of the drive towards independence and the handing over of nominal responsibility for various services to the bantustan authorities has been the elimination of such sources of official information as there used to be as regards developments inside. A common answer to the standard questions in the House of Assembly is, as in the case of health services in KwaZulu:

"Due to the fact that staff at the Hospitals concerned are on the establishment of the KwaZulu Government Service, the required information cannot be furnished."[1]

No official information seems ever to be available on a regular basis from the bantustan authorities themselves. One is therefore forced to rely on the accounts of newspaper reporters — who cover only a few aspects of some of the bantustans, mainly Transkei, Ciskei and KwaZulu, together with the squatter townships of BophuthaTswana. They can be supplemented to some extent by reports from missionary hospitals and other private organisations, but these are increasingly being taken over by officialdom and silenced. The overall effect is of massive propaganda about the politics and ceremonial of bantustan independence, concealing an almost total lack of information about conditions for the millions of people inside, and for all those being removed there from their homes in urban areas, white farms or bantustan areas which are caught up in the process of "consolidation". This chapter and the next outline some of what has emerged about the conditions these people face.

Mr. Colin Eglin, a white opposition politician, concluded from a visit to several bantustans that while independence was the "grand illusion" there, poverty was the grim reality. He observed that because of the constant deportation of people from urban areas to the bantustans without means of subsistence, the overall effect is that real per capita income in the bantustans — already among the lowest on the African continent — is falling still lower.[2]

Estimates of per capita income in the bantustans are imprecise and inconsistent. It is reported, however, that the average income in the four largest bantustans in 1974 was R7 per month, or R84 ($97) per year. This compares unfavourably with many other African countries for which figures are available, including Nigeria ($180 p.a.) Zambia ($310), Cameroon ($165), Congo ($281), Ivory Coast ($387), Liberia ($197), Central African Republic ($122), Malawi ($130), Tanzania ($120) and others. Those with a lower per capita income than the bantustans are in the drought-stricken Sahel region, the equally arid Horn of Africa, and the overcrowded mountains of Rwanda and Burundi.[3] The trend in bantustan incomes is clear, even though statistics on various sources of income, and total population, are intermittent and unreliable. The Tomlinson Commission found that from 1936 to 1954 the real income in the reserves had remained almost unaltered, while due to population growth — at that time mainly from natural increases — income per capita had fallen. According to this source, annual income per capita in the reserves in 1954, excluding the remittances of migrant workers, was R25.80[4]; if income from the white areas is included, the figure would be R48 per annum. A further estimate in 1960 gave the possible range of incomes as between R14 and R26 per annum.[5] It appears therefore that there was a net decline in actual income over those six years; taking inflation into account, the decline in real income per capita was considerable. This trend is confirmed by a 1969 estimate, which gave the per capita income as R22 per annum, of which the cash income was R15 per annum. With earnings sent in from the white areas, the level is brought up to R53 per annum; taking inflation into account, the real income again fell noticeably. In fact inflation appears to be at a higher level in the bantustans than in the white areas; from September 1973 to September 1974 the rate was almost double at 14% in the bantustans as compared with 8% in South Africa as a whole.[6]

The effects of deepening poverty can be seen in the local hospitals and similar institutions, and through analysis of whatever statistics are available. Available figures indicate for example that African men are not living as long as they used to.[7] Reports of malnutrition among all sections of the population, but particularly children, are becoming increasingly frequent. Kupugani, a voluntary organisation aimed at boosting nutrition, circulated a request for information on conditions in the bantustans at the end of 1972. The responses indicate that hundreds of people in the Transkei, Ciskei and Namaqualand are starving. Malnutrition was reported as the rule; 75–80% of the children examined at two hospitals in Pondoland, in the Transkei, were found to be suffering from it. Many of the children died or were permanently brain-damaged as a result.[8] It is widely recognised that apart from increasing poverty, the forced system of migrant labour, which involves the separation of families from their major income earner and the destruction of traditional family and community responsibilities, is a major cause of the starvation and disease in the bantustans. Dr. Trudi Thomas, who has practised for 25 years in the Ciskei, has found a strong correlation between the cohesion of families and the health and survival rate of their children. "Practically all malnourished children come from broken homes — and it is migrant labour which is breaking up their homes." The growing numbers of illegitimate children born under conditions of constant migration and the breakdown of traditional authority are those most affected by acute deprivation. About half of all the children in the Ciskei are being stunted in their growth through malnutrition.[9] In KwaZulu, a study of malnutrition warns that it is changing the people's physique; people are becoming small, stunted and mentally enfeebled.[10]

One of the pioneer African journalists, the late Nat Nakasa, visited many of the mission hospitals in KwaZulu, which has a tradition of outspoken medical personnel, during one of its drought years. He found that everywhere, the hospitals were full of children suffering from common diseases like measles and whooping cough, which in hundreds of cases killed them because of the debilitating effect of malnutrition and hunger. Only a tiny fraction of the malnourished children were reaching the hospitals, however, and it was obvious that large numbers were dying throughout the bantustan. Medical care was not the answer because the lack of food meant that children who were saved once might return several times to the hospital with the same condition; doctors battled to save children from death for the second and third times. One doctor summarised the results: "Some die and some live, but most of them die."[11]

The struggle for subsistence

These kinds of conditions are reminiscent of the drought years in the Sahel, and caused by the same kind of process of ecological breakdown — although in the case of South Africa, a much wealthier and more fertile region, the cause is government policy in crowding more and more people into the old native reserves in the name of the bantustans. As early as 1954 the Tomlinson Commission, set up to provide a blueprint for the new Nationalist policy, found that 30% of all reserve land was already "badly eroded" and another 44% "moderately eroded"; it recommended that the soil and vegetation could only be saved if the population density was reduced immediately by half in order to slow down the process of deterioration.[12] As one of the official scientific committees had earlier reported, in 1948:

"The indisputable and alarming fact is that there has been serious deterioration of the vegetable and hydrological conditions. And everywhere there has been almost terrifying erosion of the soil."[13]

By the early 1970's it had become clear that most of the area involved was out of the question for agriculture because of extreme aridity, poor fertility and steep slopes. Only 15% of QwaQwa is suitable for farming, and much of that used for resettlement camps.[14] Describing the KwaZulu bantustan, the Institute for Social Research at the University of Natal summed it up:

"If the factors of excessive slope and low rainfall alone are considered, about 70% of the areas of the Bantu reserves can be regarded as land of poor quality and generally unsuited to cultivation."[15]

Also referring to KwaZulu, a leading conservationist and environmentalist at Natal University, Professor John Hanks, warned at a series of seminars in 1978 that the condition of the soil was deteriorating rapidly. Overgrazing had stripped all vegetation from large areas, erosion was proceeding fast, and about 200 million tons of top soil were washing annually into the sea. Because of the pressure on the land, demanding crops like sugar-cane were being planted right up to the banks of the rivers, eliminating the riverine bush and allowing each of the regular floods to wash away more of the fields. With a continually rising population and disappearing topsoil, the area could face a prolonged period of real famine such as had already been observed during abnormally dry years.[16] Even the South African government's own Corporation for Economic Development (CED) has forecast a critical food shortage in the bantustans.[17]

Ecological failure, far from prompting the South African authorities to reduce overcrowding in the bantustans, is actually accompanied by an accelerating rate of increase in population densities as increasingly numbers of people are forced into the areas concerned. Already, the density in the bantustans is almost the highest in Africa, despite the fact that South Africa as a whole is relatively sparsely populated. Compared with a density of 41 per square mile in Kenya, for example, and 63 in Lesotho — which is geographically similar to the Transkei — the average density of African population in the bantustans generally was 119 per square mile in 1970, and 122 in the Transkei. The only one with less than 100 people per square mile was BophuthaTswana, which contains much desert and semi-desert, with 61.[18] Overall population density for the rest of South Africa was 35 per square mile.[19]

Between the 1960 and 1970 census the population of the bantustans increased from 4 million to 6.9 million, more than double what it had been at the time the Tomlinson Commission recommended urgent measures to reduce the numbers.[20] Since 1970, the process has continued. Table 3 shows the increase in density in each of the bantustans between 1970 and the end of 1976 — particularly startling in the case of QwaQwa, where the population almost quadrupled in that time.

Table 3 — **Population densities in the bantustans** (per hectare)

bantustan	1970[1]	1976 (end)[2]
BophuthaTswana	24.1	30.4
Ciskei	66.4	89.1
Gazunkulu	40.8	49.3
KaNgwane	—	—
KwaZulu	68.5	86.8
Lebowa	50.1	63.1
QwaQwa	50.7	189.6
Swazi	56.7	56.5
Transkei	47.2	58.3
Venda	45.1	52.2

The comparable density for the rest of South Africa (all population groups) is 13.7[1]

NB: 1970 figures are for total population, 1976 ones for Africans only. All recent South African statistics conform to the metric system.

Sources
1. Census figures given by the Minister of Statistics, *Debates*, 13.2.76.
2. Based on figures for total African population and area of the bantustans given in Table 1.

These are average figures and overcrowding is much higher in certain areas. In KwaZulu for example three districts have estimated population densities of more than 3,000 people per square mile of arable land.

What this overcrowding means in terms of human suffering can be seen by looking at the Nqutu district of Natal. The government-appointed Tomlinson Commission estimated in 1954 that the Nqutu district, if "fully developed agriculturally",

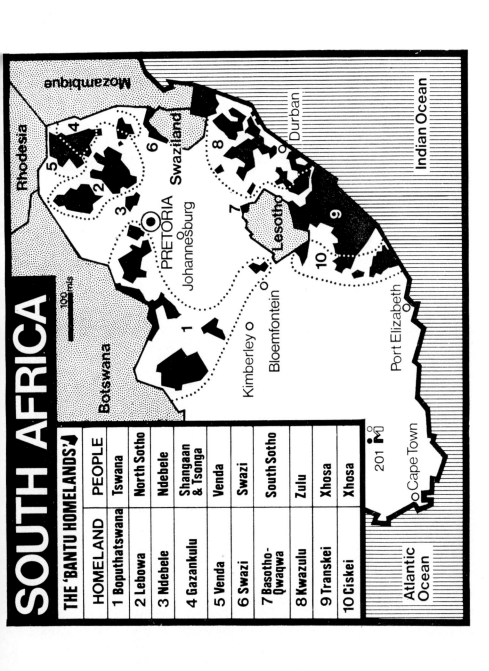

SOUTH AFRICA

THE 'BANTU HOMELANDS'

HOMELAND	PEOPLE
1 Boputhatswana	Tswana
2 Lebowa	North Sotho
3 Ndebele	Ndebele
4 Gazankulu	Shangaan & Tsonga
5 Venda	Venda
6 Swazi	Swazi
7 Basotho-Qwaqwa	South Sotho
8 Kwazulu	Zulu
9 Transkei	Xhosa
10 Ciskei	Xhosa

Mozambique

Rhodesia

Botswana

Swaziland

PRETORIA

Johannesburg

Lesotho

Kimberley

Bloemfontein

Durban

Indian Ocean

Port Elizabeth

Cape Town

Atlantic Ocean

100 mls

201

could adequately support only 13,000 people, as opposed to the 30,000 already there in 1951. However the population of Nqutu has risen phenomenally without any significant agricultural development since 1954. Through removals and other increases, by 1974 there were an estimated 80,000 people in the district and, apart from agriculture, there were only 1050 job opportunities in the area, almost half of them with the local hospital. In their book *Women Without Men: a study of 150 families in the Nqutu district of KwaZulu* Clarke and Ngobese estimated that 120,000 people would be living in Nqutu by 1980. However, in February 1979 doctors at the local Charles Johnson Memorial Hospital estimated that the population had already reached 200,000—an indication of the effects of the government's forced resettlement programme.[21]

The contrast between some of the reserve land as it could be, and what has happened to it under the bantustan policy, is striking. It has been estimated that, if properly farmed by a small enough number of people, the Transkei could produce 50 million bags of maize a year, or almost the entire consumption of South Africa. In 1970, only 1.25 million bags were produced, which was inadequate even for local needs. Over twice that amount, 2.8 million bags, had to be brought into the Transkei.[22] Where all the available resources have to be spent outside the area, in an attempt to maintain the subsistence level, it is impossible to accumulate local capital reserves for development. Chief Matanzima admitted this in his 1970 budget speech:

"The agricultural production of the Transkei has barely increased—if it has increased at all—during the last 30 years and we seem to be making little headway towards a more viable economy."[23]

Agricultural production seems to have been declining ever since the beginning of the native reserve policy in South Africa, largely because of the confinement of increasing numbers of Africans into increasingly small areas. In the 1923-27 period, 620 million pounds of maize and 148 million pounds of sorghum were produced in the reserves; in 1935-39, production was down to 478 million pounds and 122 million pounds respectively, a decline of about 20% in just over a decade.[24] Between 1958 and 1968 production of maize fell from 252,000 tons to 151,000 tons a year, a 40% drop, and sorghum fell from 45,700 tons to 22,700 tons, a fall of over 50%.[25]

During the last few years, agricultural production has been boosted by the introduction of cash crops for consumption outside the bantustans, produced by various agencies of the South African government mainly on land acquired for the bantustans in the "consolidation" process. This has boosted overall figures but does not reflect the trend in subsistence agriculture, which is the source of food and income for the people themselves. Official figures released in 1974 show total crop and pastoral production in the bantustans to have increased by 90% in the five years 1968-1973. However, the improvement was concentrated in a limited number of areas, those run on commercial lines by white managers, with little or no participation by the general population. Meanwhile in Venda, crop production dropped more than 80%, and pastoral production by more than 68%; in Gazankulu crop

49

production dropped 14.5% and pastoral production 26.5%; in the Transkei pastoral production dropped by 30%—partly as a result of a major drought.[26]

The most important items for the African subsistence economy are maize and sorghum. The productivity of white farms in these crops is well over ten times that of the bantustans, and the difference has been growing rapidly since World War II as a result of the major expenditure by the government on all aspects of white farming, and underdevelopment of African farming by crowding more people onto eroded land. The comparative figures are shown in Table 4.

Table 4:

Production of African staples in white areas and the bantustans (millions of bags)

Item		1947-8	1967-8	% change
Maize:	white areas	30.4	105.2	+246
	bantustans	3.8	3.7	−2.6
Sorghum:	white areas	1.8	9.5	+428
	bantustans	1.2	0.7	−41.7

Source: Financial Mail, 4 October 1968.

The poorest of the poor—landless people in the bantustans

Under South African law, Africans have no absolute rights in land even if they and their families have owned it for generations, or they have actually paid for it under white laws. Many farms bought by Africans in the nineteenth century have now been declared "black spots" and the people subjected to forcible removal to the nearest bantustan—with no absolute right to compensation for the value of the land, often considerable. Where bantustan land is exchanged for white land in the interests of "consolidation", the people evicted from the area are not entitled to compensation in the new area, even if they are resettled there: white farms bought to add to the bantustans are owned and operated by government agencies, while many are being leased back to white farmers despite being theoretically part of an African reserve. Another major factor in regard to land ownership is that women, who form the majority of able-bodied adults and have always been more important in farming than men, have virtually no rights to land under South African law.

Another procedure which involves moving people off the land they farm is the programme of "planning" or "rehabilitation". In order to squeeze more and more people into a given area and in the attempt to rationalise agriculture, the government authorities are engaged in a profound dislocation of local patterns of life and work, bringing scattered groups together in one area, allocating new fields for crops and for pasture, and drastically culling stock—which meets fierce resistance since in the absence of land ownership, animals are the sole form of security for bantustan farmers. This presents a classic case of "development" strategies long since discredited among international experts as basically destructive: investment in animals, housing, fencing, farmed areas and other assets is destroyed, and a major element of insecurity introduced which is a disincentive to any new investment.

The policy has provoked fierce resistance even in many normally quiet areas of the bantustans. The complaint is, as expressed by Prof. Ntsanwisi of Gazankulu:
"The homelands still belong to the central government. They allocate and reallocate land and people at will, without ever looking at the energy and money used by the people to establish themselves."[27]

The response of the authorities, as expressed by the chief Agricultural Officer of the Transkei, is that "compulsion will have to be resorted to."[28] This has been a running battle since the beginning of the programme in 1945, and in many cases the police have been called in to put down riots and enforce the removal of people according to the plan. In one recent case, police called in to protect inspectors sent to register cattle prior to culling fired on a crowd of protesting Africans, killing two and wounding four.[29] The Transkei Minister of Agriculture described the incident:
"They slashed the tyres of the drilling machines, and tried to burn them out. Fences were destroyed and the lives of agricultural officers threatened . . . "

A Transkei politician, the late Curnick Ndamse, commented that "the question of agriculture and all that goes with it has become dynamite."[30] No progress in agricultural production is observable in "planned areas", and such is the antipathy towards the planning policy that even the major irrigation schemes are lying disused because people cannot be persuaded to join the scheme in spite of the financial incentives involved.[31]

The process of removing bantustan people from their land and replacing them with government agencies or white farmers is to continue and be greatly expanded, according to the South African government's policy for agriculture in the bantustans announced in July 1973. Land ownership, even in the "planned" areas, is not to be vested in African farmers, as proposed by the Tomlinson Commission, but in the bantustan "governments". European agency participation is to be greatly expanded in relation to cash crops such as sugar, cotton, coffee and sisal, using bantustan land. And, as a corollary to this master plan, "excess farmers" will be resettled in the bantustan townships; the Deputy Minister of Bantu Development stated that he would like to see the present number of 500,000 small farmers in the bantustans reduced to 50,000, or at most 100,000. This would mean that the overwhelming majority of the bantustan population would be landless. As Mr. Raubenheimer declared, it is government policy that the idea that every member of a bantustan community is entitled to a piece of its land is to "fall away".[32]

Landlessness can mean no income at all, either in cash or in kind. In a survey of households in various Transkei villages, it was found that 95% of all households had a cash income of under R50 (£28) a month, mainly migrant workers' remittances, which is well below the subsistence level; 50% had under R12 (£7) a month.[33] With a government policy of making most people completely landless, the problem of bare physical survival comes into prominence for increasing numbers of households. To some extent it is a mystery how people with no cash income and no source of food such as land or livestock survive, even now; the answer, according to local observers, is the willingness of those who have a little to share with those who have nothing, since life is so insecure inside the bantustans that all are well aware that they too may need such help at anytime. Thus the burden of absolute poverty is spread around the community as a whole, particularly if it has a strong local identity. With the disruption of traditional communities, which are firmly tied to the soil they work, and the massive increase in landlessness, it is an open question how long such a survival mechanism can continue.

Conflict

An inevitable result of destitution inside the bantustans is that people living on the edges raid the surrounding white-owned farms for food, water and fodder for their animals. The situation along the innumerable borders is tense, with confrontation reaching the level of open warfare. One farmer, Dolf Pienaar, whose farm is bordered by the Lebowa bantustan, considers himself at war with its inhabitants and is preparing for a "fight to the finish". Every year he takes a tractor into the bantustan to pull down earthen dams the people have built for water from streams which he considers his: "What can I do but take the law into my own hands?" At night, he alleges, the people tear down his fences and bring their cattle into his farm to feed. They also construct "landmines" out of heavy wire which puncture the tyres of his truck. Dolf's response is violent: "I have seven rifles in my house, and I am always ready to use them. I am fighting to stay alive."[34] Much more, it seems, are the people of the bantustan.

This picture is apparently typical of the bantustan borders. The white farmers concerned have expressed strong concern at the deteriorating situation on border farms in the Eastern Cape, around the Ciskei and Transkei. Various problems were listed: stock theft, intimidation of staff, "trespassing" and general confrontation. A farmer calling for strong action at the Eastern Agricultural Union suggested that all bantustans should be fenced in before becoming independent, and that a no-man's-land be created between the borders and the nearest farms. Another farmer suggested that the army be called in to patrol the borders.[35]

Violence is not by any means a new phenomenon in the bantustans; its character is changing, however, as the bantustan structures are reinforced. Cosmas Desmond has described the change:

"There have been rebellions against authority in the rural areas before; but as the government sets up the screen of Bantu Authorities between itself and the people, the immediate symbols of apartheid in the Reserves will more and more be Africans. Violence directed against oppression will appear as internal tribal strife."[36]

This is indeed the case, as seen from the South African press; the major confrontations in the bantustans are reported either as "faction fights" or as having no apparent reason. They tend to be associated with stock thefts and disputes over land, especially in areas which are being "planned," with the best land going to those villages which collaborate with the authorities; alternatively, they are in areas where people are being removed, either because the government has allocated them to different bantustans or because of consolidation. The KwaZulu area of Msinga is a particularly explosive one, and it is here that many deportees from white areas are being settled in camps or on tiny land allocations.

It is impossible to estimate the extent of fighting in the bantustans, since only the Transkei and KwaZulu receive much press attention and individual murders or attacks involving a few dead and wounded may well not be reported to the police, let alone become known to the press in the cities. From those cases that are known, however, it is evident that this is becoming an increasingly serious aspect of bantustan life, not only in the form of "faction fights" between communities, but also as riots in the schools. Mission hospitals in the Transkei regard the trauma arising out of these conflicts to be the major medical problem that they have to deal with, even compared with the high levels of malnutrition and disease.[37]

There has been violent opposition to the bantustan authorities and figureheads in the Transkei ever since it was set up as the first model for "separate development" in the early 1960s.[38] In 1973 Chief Matanzima claimed that "terrorist organisations" were recruiting men in the Transkei.[39] It is known that secret organisations dating back to the early sixties such as "The Hill," were still operating in Pondoland and possibly elsewhere.[40]

One "faction fight" in the Libode district of the Transkei led to 275 arrests; at least 40 bodies were later recovered.[41] The fighting overall was so bad that the matron of St. Barnabas Hospital wrote:

". . . there are many families who are actually starving — many due to the recent faction fights."[42]

At Cofimvaba High School, in 1973, about 130 pupils were arrested after a riot in which a pupil was shot, a car overturned, the principal's house sacked and a shop looted. One of the reasons was found to be fear of the coming examinations for which they had not received textbooks and stationery, or adequate teaching.[43] It seems that the leaders of the riots are usually children sent to the bantustan schools because official policy prohibited them from attending schools at home, in the cities.[44] Also in 1973, a series of battles between rival villages in Eastern Pondoland resulted in nine deaths. In a nearby area, the Flagstaff district, a tribal clash developed into a scorched earth operation, with about 60 houses burnt down and grazing destroyed over a large area. Another battle in January 1974 led to five dead and several injured, also in Eastern Pondoland.[45] A series of fights at big beer-drinking parties in different areas at the end of 1974 led to another 10 dead and many injured and arrested.[46]

In KwaZulu, there has been violence at Msinga lasting for several years and leading to the imposition of a state of emergency. Chief Buthelezi specifically requested the imposition of emergency powers, in response to "savagery" and "terrorism"; he claimed that "criminals" were in control of the district. There had been 69 murders, 31 attempted murders, 213 serious assaults and 529 cases of stock theft, as well as 921 huts burned down between January 1971 and January

1972.[47] Later in 1972 further fighting broke out, leading to 40 deaths.[48] The feuding spread to Soweto, where people had links with the communities involved, and in 1974 at least 20 men were reported to have been killed there and in Kwa-Zulu.[49]

Elsewhere in KwaZulu there has also been violence. More than 100 pupils at the KwaDlangelwa High School rioted in 1973, threatening teachers and smashing rooms. Police shot one girl and injured several others in a baton charge.[50] In the same year, as part of a long-standing feud an old chief was killed near Eshowe and 8 huts burned down.[51] Fierce fighting in various places at the end of the year resulted in at least 21 deaths.[52] In 1974 fighting broke out in the Ingwavuma region between supporters of rival claimants to a chieftainship. Between 400 and 500 families fled the scene of the fighting; later, at least seven were murdered, and hundreds of people left homeless. This was the latest in a series of clashes which included the stealing and maiming of cattle and burning of huts.[53] In early 1975 one person was hacked to death and three others seriously injured in a fight in the Impendle district. A feature of this and many of the other clashes is that people were heavily armed while going to ostensibly peaceful gatherings.

1976, the year of the massive disturbances in Soweto and other urban centres, was also a time of much less well-known violence inside the bantustans, involving practically every one of them. The issues have been the same as in the towns — protests against Bantu Education and the *apartheid* system generally — but with the added dimension of resistance to the bantustan authorities and their South African backers. In the Ciskei, for example, there was a trail of violent protest in 1977 involving a flare-up among young people who attacked Ciskei government buildings and cars, at about the same time as the violence related to the funeral of Steve Biko in neighbouring KingWilliamsTown.[54] Immediately afterwards, five hundred young people set fire to the offices of the Ciskei Department of Labour in Dimbaza, as well as other offices, an official vehicle and a school.[55] The following month the houses of two Ciskei police were attacked and a post office gutted. Schools were attacked, and pupils boycotted classes.[56] A car belonging to a councillor of the Zwelitsha township was burned, destroying records of the proceedings of the former Ciskei Territorial Authority.[57] All these incidents were accompanied by violent clashes with the police, who used tear-gas, batons and shot several people during the confrontations. At a meeting where the Ciskei Chief Minister, Chief Lennox Sebe, urged parents to make their children go to school, he reacted with fury to hecklers; a group of men was called to deal with the opponents and sticks and heavy sjamboks (whips) were used to silence them.[58] Opposition continued despite the police attacks, however; early in 1978 several school classsrooms were burned down together with a house which held the administrative offices of the Ciskeian Government in Port Elizabeth.[59] During the Ciskei elections there were serious clashes involving burning, looting and several injuries.[60] Other fights occurred during election meetings.[61]

A rather similar series of clashes occurred at the same time in Venda; two people were believed to have died in a "rampage" by school pupils in the bantustan in October 1977 which resulted in expensive and extensive damage to school buildings.[62] The scale of the disturbances is indicated by the fact that more than 12,000 pupils had been sent home indefinitely because of the "very bad" atmosphere in the schools.[63] A crowd of about 16,000 demonstrating students had stoned the car of Venda's Chief Minister, Chief Patrick Mphephu, in the Venda capital of Sibasa during a demonstration against Bantu Education. Mphephu was forced to flee for his life, and there were violent confrontations. Three houses belonging to Venda police were burnt, and the homes of Venda cabinet ministers and officials, the Legislative Assembly and the Venda Development Corporation were all attacked.[64]

At Mahla in Gazankulu, the home of the white principal of the Oribilani High School was stoned and the school itself set alight, causing damage of more than R3,000 (£1,700). Police arrested about 125 schoolchildren marching on the magistrate's offices.[65] Similar unrest was reported from QwaQwa, where school pupils boycotted classes; at the same time a petrol bomb was thrown at the house of the QwaQwa Minister of Education.[66] In the Transkei, areas which had been relatively quiet since 1975 erupted into vicious "faction" fighting in 1978, with seven people killed. The local Commissioner of Police at first denied any knowledge of the battle, but when a reporter confronted him with the facts he admitted it, but denied it had been a faction fight.[67] It seems likely to have been connected with the political conflicts occurring at the time, but no official admission was available about this connection.

More information has appeared in the press about BophuthaTswana and KwaZulu, where violence has been almost endemic. The opposition to Mangope's decision to opt for "independence" has been described in chapter 3; Mangope and four of his Cabinet Ministers only narrowly escaped serious injury in one stoning incident.[68] Like Venda, BophuthaTswana had its Legislative Assembly building attacked.[69] There have also been a series of attacks on bantustan officials, vehicles and buildings, many of which were burned to the ground. Massive damage was also caused to a new shopping and business complex in a township near Pretoria, only just opened by Chief Mangope.[70] The *Rand Daily Mail* saw the arson and violence as an expression of fury at the official system:

". . . there is little doubt a cardinal fact was the feeling among African youth that the homeland governments are part and parcel of the apartheid system. Hence a blow against a homeland government is seen as a blow against apartheid."[71]

At the same time, there were unpremeditated attacks of great violence, as in the case of a white hunter from Pretoria savagely beaten by a mob in BophuthaTswana.[72] A school soccer game in the bantustan turned unexpectedly into a battle, with 23 students knifed or beaten.[73] Among older people, there were vicious "faction fights" over political control in the Maboloka area; many people were killed, houses set on fire and people forced to flee. Administration broke down to the point where people were not able to get the necessary permission to bury their dead.[74]

KwaZulu has seen terrible faction fighting, involving knives, guns and other lethal weapons. In one particular trouble spot, Msinga, 94 people were killed in these battles between 1972 and early 1976, with 1,802 homes destroyed.[75] In a single Christmas weekend at the end of 1976, at least 88 people died in faction fights and related murders.[76] In some cases people were shot dead attempting to escape from their burning homes.[77] The full death toll is probably much higher than the official count, since the victorious group usually buries the bodies of their enemies soon after the battle.[78] Violence has continued unabated, and has become so deeply entrenched around Msinga that villagers often sleep in the hills coming down to their fields only in daylight. This obviously increases still further the difficulties of scratching a subsistence living; but the violence is itself a product of the poverty and dislocation caused by crowding people into the bantustans. Neil Alcock, who runs a church-sponsored agricultural community project on the edge of the Msinga area, asserts:

"The fighting is largely an expression of frustration by people who have been deprived of any access to a livelihood. Before people were removed from white farms and dumped in Msinga, things were relatively peaceful."[79]

20,000 people have been forced into resettlement areas with only half an acre each and forced to give up their cattle. Two of the main factions involved in the violence are the Majolas and the Madondos, both of which were moved eight years previously from white farms into KwaZulu; the battles between them are at least in part a struggle for the impoverished land.[80] Those detained have no means of raising bail; relatives who went to Johannesburg to earn money for the purpose were themselves attacked as the fighting spread into Soweto.[81] In 1978 "execution squads" based in KwaZulu were reported to be operating in Johannesburg.[82] 23 people were known to have been killed, many of these badly multilated, in the extension of KwaZulu faction fighting on the Reef in the first eight months of that year.[83]

The situation in KwaZulu has deteriorated so far that a kind of mob rule prevails. Gangs thrive on stock thefts, backed up by intimidation and murder, complete with summary condemnation of people in their own 'kangaroo courts', according to Neil Alcock. The police are almost totally ineffective in preventing thefts, which leave people destitute; even if missing animals are found the owners are liable to be attacked by the thieves.[84] Particularly vulnerable to attack are the women, who face abduction, rape and serious injury at the hands of men and, more recently, boys.[85] Women are also the target for men of opposing factions, who are likely to attack them whenever their male relatives are absent or in jail.

KwaZulu has also seen attacks on the bantustan authorities, indicative of the unsettled and violent atmosphere. In 1977 a member of the Legislative Assembly was shot dead.[86] In 1978 a flash school riot, described as "spontaneous" by the head of the police investigation team, led to one teacher being stoned to death and another seriously stabbed.[87] A little later the brother of the KwaZulu Minister of Justice was killed by a gang outside his own house.[88] Such incidents are illustrative of the state of civil unrest which prevails in many bantustan areas.

CHAPTER 6

Removals

"Behind the 'self-government' talks (for the bantustans) lies a grim programme of mass evictions, political persecution and police terror", wrote Nelson Mandela in 1959.[1]

The categories of people who are officially intended to live permanently in the bantustans include almost all African women, as well as the unemployed, the old, the sick and most children. These are the people whom the Deputy Minister of Bantu Administration described in 1969 as the 'superfluous appendages' of African workers.[2]

In practice the forced removal of people to the bantustans is composed to a large extent of the dumping of women. For South African officials, such rights as may be available to Africans are for men: the most important of these is the right to earn a living, however meagre, in the white areas. Many more work permits are given to African men than to women. African men are basic to the paid labour force in South Africa; African women are considered redundant. Most African women are defined as minors, i.e. as children, who cannot in their own right enter into contracts, travel without permission of their male relatives, own property — apart from personal effects — or retain any earnings they may have, since these are vested in their guardians and may be attached by the men's creditors.[3] As already mentioned, women are not usually allowed any rights to land in the bantustans for themselves and their dependants, who include large numbers of old people, the sick, mentally and physically handicapped, and increasing numbers of unemployed men. A married woman whose husband dies or deserts her (a common phenomenon under the system of migrant labour) may lose her right to work the land she has farmed for years. This is of increasing importance as women are top priority for removal from urban areas, the men being moved from family homes to enormous men-only barracks.

Almost two million people were moved to the bantustans between 1960 and 1970, as shown in Table 5. In 1969 Mr. Froneman estimated that another 3.8 million "superfluous Bantu", most of them women, were still to be moved from the white urban areas.[4] Judging from the projected size of new bantustan township camps for landless people, to house migrant workers and their families, a further 4 million people were on the list for removal during the next few years, both from the white areas and from land-owning communities practising sub-subsistence agriculture inside the bantustans.[5] These figures seem to exclude those affected by consolidation programmes, and also by "planning", which means the removal of people from the traditional scattered homesteads, or kraals, into large villages with fenced pasture and crop-lands.

Table 5 — **Removals 1960-1970**

Number of persons moved	Reason
340,000	Abolition of labour tenancies on white farms.
656,000	Laws prohibiting squatters living on white farms.
97,000	Elimination of "black spots" in the rural areas.*
400,000	"Endorsement out" of the urban areas under pass law offences and other legislation controlling the lives of urban Africans (particularly the Bantu Laws Amendment Act of 1964).
327,000	Resiting of urban townships in the neighbouring reserves.
TOTAL: 1,820,000	

*A further 69,000 are still to be removed from "black spots".
Source: SA Institute of Race Relations: "Some Notes on the Size and Distribution of the African Population." (14.2.72).

This strategy which began on a smaller scale in the 1950's was attacked by ANC leader Nelson Mandela as a policy of deliberate impoverishment:

"The main object is to create a huge army of migrant labourers, domiciled in rural locations in the reserves far away from the cities. Through the implementation of the scheme it is hoped that in the course of time the inhabitants of the reserves will be uprooted and completely severed from their land, cattle and sheep, to depend for their livelihood entirely on wage earnings."[6]

By 1974, according to the Deputy Minister of Bantu Development, well over half of the total bantustan area had been "planned" the land divided up by officials and people moved in accordance with the plan. A breakdown of the numbers is given in Table 6. It seems that over 4 million people have been moved out of their homes under this planning programme, and the remaining 2.8 million are likely to be moved, since the "development" objective is to plan the entire area.

The proposals for "consolidation" announced in 1972-73 have also meant large-scale removals, this time of people actually living inside bantustans who have in many cases already been subject to two, three or even more removals.

Estimates of the numbers of Africans to be removed in terms of the consolidation plan seem to be at best sketchy. No official estimate was given when the "first phase" of the Ciskei consolidation plan was announced in 1972. The consolidation of BophuthaTswana is officially estimated to involve the removal of 80,000 people in the Transvaal and 40,000 in the Cape while the plans for KwaZulu, Lebowa, Gazankulu, Ka Ngwane, Ndebele and Venda are officially estimated to involve

Table 6 — **Percentage of total area planned**

Bantustan	Percentage planned	Total population	Number of people moved*
BophuthaTswana	56.1	884,000	496,000
Ciskei	78.8	524,000	413,000
Gazankulu	99.0	267,000	264,000
KwaZulu	49.1	2,096,000	1,029,000
Lebowa	65.0	1,084,000	705,000
Qwaqwa	100.0	25,000	25,000
Transkei	59.5	1,734,000	1,032,000
Venda	77.6	264,000	205,000
			TOTAL: 4,169,000

*It is assumed that the number of people affected is proportional to the percentage of land planned. In fact this is possibly an underestimate, since it is the most overcrowded areas that receive priority in rehabilitation.

Sources: Percentages of total area planned by 1974 given by the Deputy Minister of Bantu Development in reply to a question in the House of Assembly; *Debates,* 8 February, 1974, col. 8. Total population figures derived from figures given in Table 1. All population figures rounded to the nearest 1,000.

231,000 people in the Transvaal and 132,000 in Natal. Thus, the official estimate for removals, excluding the Ciskei, is a total of 483,000 people. This is regarded by several observers, however, as a substantial underestimate. Chief Mangope of BophuthaTswana, for example, estimated that the plans would involve resettling at least 250,000 people in his bantustan instead of the 120,000 given by the government.[7] The removals in Natal alone are estimated by an opposition member of Parliament to involve 300,000 people,[8] as compared to the 132,000 estimated by the Government. Since the unofficial estimates are more than double the official ones, it would seem that the number of Africans to be removed from what they had been told to regard as their "homeland" is about one million. This is in addition to the 209,000 Africans already moved under the bantustan consolidation plan from April 1968 to June 1971, and those removed before and since this time.[9]

It would seem, then, that a total of about 13.9 million Africans could be involved in these removal programmes under the bantustan policy. Around 6.3 million have already been moved, and another 7.7 million are on the list. In a number of cases these figures will refer to the same people who may be moved several times in terms of different aspects of the bantustan policy, or changes in the policy and the constantly shifting outlines of the bantustans themselves. Not only must Africans be in a bantustan; it must be the "correct" one. If the bantustan area they are in changes its name, they have no lasting home there. It is hard to grasp the meaning of this in human terms. Certain common features stand out in the available reports, however.[10]

One is the misrepresentation of the places to which people are to be moved as fertile, well-watered and with full facilities. Mr. M. C. Botha has claimed:

"The Bantu people like being moved . . . The Bantu people like the places where they are being resettled."[11]

A typical instance is the removal at short notice of some families who owned land at Rietfontein near Lichtenburg, to BophuthaTswana. The Department of Bantu Administration and Development claimed: "The people of Rietfontein volunteered to go to De Hoop; in fact they said we were too slow in moving them." In fact, according to the local chief the removal was abrupt, preventing the people from harvesting their fields; compensation was promised but never paid, the new location was further from employment and medical facilities, and the promised clinic, church and school had not been built.[12]

In numerous cases, the people have refused to move voluntarily in spite of the promised advantages. In these cases, if they own the land, the South African Government can simply expropriate it.[13] The people's spokesmen can be jailed, as happened for example to the Chieftainess of the Pedi people when their own farm was declared a "black spot". The Pedi people were reported to be deeply resentful, and few were willing to move; following a deadline set by the authorities, officials brought trucks to move people, accompanied by armed police. Belongings were loaded on, and homes demolished.[14] 2,000 people who had lived for several generations on another farm labelled a "black spot" also refused to move to Lebowa, on the grounds that the area provided was too small. The police dragged the chief from his home, arrested him and four others, and used tear gas to disperse the angry crowd. The people were moved and their homes bulldozed.[15] This pattern is repeated with monotonous regularity, with people forcibly moved and their homes destroyed, usually without compensation; on arrival at the new site, in spite of various promises they find no accommodation except sometimes tents, inadequate water supplies and sanitation, and none of the facilities which they have left such as schools, churches and clinics. In South Sotho, the Central Board spoke of an "explosive atmosphere" and "incitement to hostility" during the Thaba'Nchu removals in 1974 — although Chief Mangope of BophuthaTswana, from where they were being taken, had claimed that the people were "moving of their own free will."[16] In KwaZulu the then executive councillor for community affairs, Mr. Barney Dladla, criticised removals under the consolidation programme as being aimed to "dispossess us of everything that constitutes wealth in order to keep us in semi-slavery conditions."[17]

The passage of the 1973 Bantu Laws Amendment Act may have accelerated these massive removals, since it removed all legal grounds for resistance on the part of Africans, even whole communities, who are arbitrarily deported from their homes and land in accordance with the master plan.

The *Financial Mail* complained just before its passage: "Everything points to the blueprint having been hastily prepared by Pretoria. It neatly straightens out irregular Black-White boundaries, without regard to natural geographical dividing lines, population densities, agricultural production, strategic realities or — and most important of all — the future economy . . .

"It is a generator of ill-will and could reap a bitter harvest."[18]

In general, the consolidation proposals have been adjusted largely to accommodate particular white interest groups, especially the farmers. A senior government official, who has been working with the Swazi people on the basis of promises that the bantustan areas were to be their "homeland," has said:

"It is a complete betrayal of trust. The Africans have been told for nearly 40 years: 'This is your land. It will be safe for you to build here, to establish your families, to invest in schools and businesses and churches.' Now that is all to be taken away. The effect on the people will be disastrous."

He added that by excising Nsikaze, the major part of KaNgwane, the Government would be extending the migrant labour system "with its hostels, abandoned families, and other evils."[19]

In KwaZulu, although the government needed only 56,600 hectares of land to fulfil the 1936 quota, it is buying up 505,870 hectares of white land and taking 446,200 hectares of African land to fulfil its plan for "consolidation."[20]

The cost of these plans is enormous. Although little or no compensation is given to Africans deported from their homes, the cost of buying white farms is far higher than market prices, and includes an additional allowance to cover resettlement and general inconvenience.[21] In KwaZulu alone this is expected to involve a budget of R340 million.[22] There is no provision for such expenditures in the bantustan budget; it is therefore clear that the removal programme could drain the bantustan administrations even of the little they have been allocated, as well as requiring additional financing from elsewhere. It has been reported that the South African government at one stage tried to raise an overseas loan of R300 million for purchasing white farms for bantustan "consolidation."[23] The loan could well have been raised as general governmental expenditure, for which South Africa has been raising large sums on the Euro-dollar market and from European, North American and Japanese banks. The economic recession in South Africa has reprieved many Africans by leading to the drastic reduction in the budget for consolidation.

Among the recent removals, the most extensive have been in the various fragments of BophuthaTswana, in terms of an agreement between the South African government and the newly "independent" BophuthaTswana government at the end of 1977. The agreement, published in South Africa's government Gazette, covered the removal of Africans in large numbers, with the key targets being those designated as "squatters" in the Winterveldt area near Pretoria, and the Thaba 'Nchu area, a piece of land far removed from the rest of the bantustan in the Free State, containing a majority of non-"Tswanas". Under the agreement, non-"Tswanas" can be removed, and landowners who are not citizens of the bantustans in question can be expropriated if they refuse to co-operate in settlement projects. Both of the areas are inhabited mainly by people not classified as Tswanas; therefore the majority of the population is liable to removal. In another agreement, South Africa has undertaken not to hand over the township of

Mabopane East, which is near Winterveldt, to any other bantustan despite the fact that the majority of the people are not classified as Tswanas.[24] If added to BophuthaTswana, therefore, this township also will be the target of removals for the majority of people there.

Winterveldt is a general term for an area beginning about 30 km north of Pretoria and is a semi-circle around South Africa's capital with a diameter of about 80 km. Much of it is now officially in BophuthaTswana, while other bits — for no apparent reason — remain officially in the Republic of South Africa. It is this ghetto, a conglomeration of shanty towns, that provides the labour force for Pretoria and neighbouring industrial centres, including Johannesburg. Mrs. Joyce Harris, national president of the Black Sash, described Winterveldt as follows:

"Winterveldt is a slum, It exists because housing is not provided for people, because working men are expected to spend their entire working lives separated from their families, because 'unproductive Bantu' and 'superfluous appendages' are constantly being endorsed out of the white urban areas and have nowhere to go. It is a direct by-product of [South African] government policy."[25]

Winterveldt is itself a resettlement area, most of its population having been expelled from urban townships, "black spots" and white-owned farms where they worked and sometimes had small plots of their own, in the late 1960s. Winterveldt was designated a temporary reception area in 1968, when population removals of this type were at their height, and many people obtained permits to live there. The official population is some 350,000, but the local magistrate has admitted that there may be as many as 750,000 altogether, the illegal majority living in conditions even worse than the others, in areas without water supplies or sanitation.[26] Altogether some 100,000 people had been evicted from Winterveldt, or were under threat of eviction, by the beginning of 1979, many of them being moved for the second or third time. It is hardly surprising that they are demoralised by this continual process of relocation; *The Voice* reported, "there is a general spirit of apathy and hopelessness. No community solidarity apparent."[27] Once evicted, many people have absolutely nowhere to go, and they remain in Winterveldt or soon return there, where they know people. The threat of being moved on yet again is compounded by the refusal of work seekers' permits for those not classified as Tswana, the vital document allowing them to seek jobs in Pretoria and the surrounding area. One resident commented hopelessly, "Life has reached a dead end for us. With no right of a house and no work, we are just surviving only in order to die."[28] Another, a pensioner from Sophiatown, compared the people's condition to that of animals: "We have been waiting for a message from the authorities for the past eight years. There has been no promise nor even a ray of hope. We are sitting here like 'apies' (monkeys) in the veld. With no tomorrow."[29] For many others, however, there are unwelcome messages from the authorities: midnight raids to catch those illegally in the area, arrests, fines or prison, gutting of their shacks by the authorities, all compounded by widespread harrassment by criminal gangs who also raid in the middle of the night, pretending to be police.[30] In one of the raids, hundreds of people arrested were kept standing packed together for hours, including a woman in advanced pregnancy.[31] One reporter mentioned killings and maimings, saying: "an atmosphere of fear and suspicion hangs over the city."[32] People were desperate because of starvation and fear, particularly of the BophuthaTswana officials who seemed to have taken over the oppressive function of the South African police. The local police commandant admitted that his men raided houses at night, but explained: "it occurs in the normal routine of police work. It is nothing special."[33] Meanwhile the BophuthaTswana Minister of Urban Affairs and Land Tenure, Mr. D. C. Mokale, claimed not to know anything about the raids.[34] Many of the officials are growing rich on bribes as people with some money use this as a way out of the crisis; payments of R200 (£115) are cited for preferential treatment over housing permits, pensions and even state registration of marriages.[35] One elderly man, mistaking a reporter for an official, offered him R10 (£5.70) as "forgiveness money" for not yet having moved; he explained, "All the lorries were booked and we could not get one."[36] Many areas were evacuated after repeated official harrassment; at Klipgat, 30,000 people forming an established and stable community were finally forced to leave after an official ultimatum, leaving behind eight schools which had been built entirely by the local people.[37] Not even BophuthaTswana citizenship saved the people here; the South African magistrate ordering evictions had refused to allow this to be used as a mitigating factor although they were supposedly citizens in their own state.[38] By Christmas, 1978, Klipgat looked like a ghost town. The people, although they had nowhere to go to, had "vanished" as ordered, "like people from a bombed city" as *The Post* put it. Most of them, it seems, had moved to other parts of the squatter zone where they continued to be harrassed as illegal.[39] Similar stories were reported for squatter areas at Stinkwater, Majaneng and other places.[40]

For these people continually moving from one squatter area to another, conditions are grim. Even Chief Mangope, the new President of BophuthaTswana, said of it, "The conditions in the Winterveldt are such that they are a hazard to health" — although he continued to promote removal policies that contributed to the health hazards.[41] In some of the worst areas, such as the Hoekfontein district of the bantustan north of Pretoria where thousands of people were living without water or sanitation, BophuthaTswana officials refused to admit that they had any responsibility at all, claiming it to be under South African jurisdiction; the South Africans asserted that the entire responsibility lay with the bantustan. Squatters told a journalist that up to eight people were crowded into cardboard and corrugated iron hovels; that harrassment by supporters of Mangope seeking support for him was rife; and that prostitution had become a way of life.[42] In this extremely arid area there was no free water; residents were being charged as much as R2 (£1.15) a drum for it, and women said that they had been forced to prostitute themselves for water. Residents also said they were being intimidated by gangs of men patrolling with knobkieries (heavy nailed clubs) to make sure nobody told outsiders about their living conditions.[43] Conditions allowed serious corruption among the local headmen, councillors and clerks who were running extortion rackets in residence permits.[44] Reports from a number of other places indicate the lack of water; extreme cold as residents live in tents, or rickety shacks, without any protection against near-freezing night temperatures; and shacks collapsing in wind, and failing to keep out rain.[45]

It is impossible here to detail every recent removal project connected with the bantustan policy; people are moved out of, into and between bantustans according to the latest turn of the policy. One case stands out as perhaps representative of the upheavals to come as people are moved from bantustan to another in the search for tribal "purity", and the exchange of people as fragments of reserve land are taken from one bantustan to add to another — particularly one which must look respectable for its independence ceremony. The case in question is the Thaba 'Nchu area near Lesotho, which is occupied mainly by people classified as South Sotho but which is designated as part of the newly independent Bophutha-Tswana — despite the fact that there is no geographical connection with the other pieces. Following a debate behind closed doors at the Free State Congress of the National Party in September 1978, Dr. Connie Mulder, South African Minister of Plural Relations, announced a swap of land with BophuthaTswana to allow for the removal of 66,000 "South Sothos" from Thaba 'Nchu. These people outnumber the nominally Tswana population in the area by two to one.[46]

There used to be a joke that the tiny dorp of Thaba 'Nchu was such a peaceful place that for many years the local police station was staffed by only one bored constable. He was eventually transferred because there was no need for him, there were certainly no "tribal" differences between the local Tswana and the local Sotho.[47] Enormous problems were then created by South African policies which directed unwanted people from all over the Free State into their "homeland" here, with the creation of a vast and continually growing squatter camp at Kromdraai. Many of the people are old, disabled or ill, with nobody to support them. One old woman living in complete destitution probably represented many; she had been injured in a work accident on a white-owned farm, and when she came out of hospital was taken back there — but the farmer refused to accept her. The ambulance then took her to a local magistrate who applied for a disability grant for her and returned her to the farmer. She was directed to the "homeland", where grants are often not paid.[48] Other people came of their own accord, having nowhere else to go, and in 1972 removals to QwaQwa, the tiny South Sotho "homeland", began — but as fast as people were removed, new ones arrived. As *The Voice* described it:

"Big GG [South African government] lorries left Thaba 'Nchu piled high with furniture, corrugated iron and chicken wire with bewildered faces peering down . . . at weekends other lorries (and horse carts) were still arriving, similarly laden, The removals were stopped — QwaQwa had no room. Kromdraai spread out around the hill, filling every available space with corrugated iron shacks and mud-brick houses.[49]

The camp is on traditional grazing land; the locals attacked the newcomers, factions sprang up, and violence became endemic. In Kromdraai itself, conditions are so bad that police leave it alone unless strictly necessary. The BophuthaTswana officials started a "reign of terror" in 1978 aimed at getting rid of the people, and there have been a series of clashes with dawn raids, mass arrests, severe beatings of teachers taken from their school — women were hit between the legs with planks — and people shot, including one elderly woman shot in the back.[50]

Increasingly, it is the resettlement camps inside the bantustans like Kromdraai, Stinkwater and the entire Winterveldt area which are the focus of removals and the associated violence and despair. It may be that entire areas of bantustans become vast resettlement camps with little pretext about giving people land to live from, like the QwaQwa bantustan which was described by one member of its Legislative Assembly as "a concentration camp where Basotho are being dumped to live in perpetual misery."[51] A follow-up study on people moved to Limehill in KwaZulu ten years previously indicated "a general air of dilapidation, desolation and isolation about the place." There was only one water-tap to 35 families, virtually no employment, a general air of fear which extended both to the Security Police and to "communists" i.e. people opposed to government policy, whom they had been warned to report to the police. Poverty was the norm, and resulted in a high death-toll especially of children. 11% of those under 5 at the time of removals had since died, almost 20% of those born at Limehill had died; this did not include perinatal mortality, which would raise the percentage substantially. Perhaps worst of all, there was no hope and no way back to a previous way of life that had offered at least an income and a basic dignity; one respondent explained that he "had no hope that to go back would help him now and that the only thing he wants is to die and not to try anything, because whatever a Black man is saying it will become a source of death."[52] Limehill is representative of the older camps; meanwhile, their number is increasing all the time through the creation of new ones. In Ciskei, for example, are several camps which sprang up virtually overnight for somewhere between 30,000 and 50,000 people fleeing independent Transkei rule in Glen Grey and Herschel when their areas were transferred from Ciskei to Transkei on the eve of the latter's independence. The Ciskei administration, alarmed at the horror stories being filed from the makeshift camps, banned reporters from the area; but it was already admitted by officials that the mortality rate, particularly among infants, was running at around five a day. Unofficial estimates were that 300 people had died in the camps in the first three months of their operation.[53]

Official policy is that people must go to the bantustans regardless of whether they can physically survive there. Mr. Froneman announced that the South African government was under no obligation to prepare accommodation for people it was deporting from their homes: "The removal of these superfluous Bantu from the White Homelands is not dependent on the development of the Bantu Homelands." In the words of one Bantu Affairs Commissioner, the camps contain "redundant people. . . [who] could not render productive service in an urban area . . . men who had lost their jobs and could not find new employment; old and infirm people; unmarried mothers."[54] The implication is that the government has no interest in their survival. The message is clear as far as the people involved are concerned; as they told one visitor, "We have been thrown away", "We are suffering", "We have nothing", "We are only Africans, there is no one to hear us."[55]

For the South African government, however, which increasingly attributes responsibility for the camps to the bantustan authorities that it has itself appointed, the camps are a great success. In the words of the Deputy Minister of Bantu Development, "Each of these places is a manifestation of the successful implementation of the policy of separate development."[56].

CHAPTER 7

Bantustan Policies

The role of the Legislative Assemblies, or parliaments, in the bantustans is more impressive on paper than it is in reality. The opening of the Bophutha-Tswana Legislative Assembly in 1972 was described in the following press report as something of a charade:

"It has all the trappings of a real parliament . . . including robes, procession and mace. The huge majority of the Chief Minister's party sit crammed in one side—many fidgeting, some sleeping. Eight opposition members on the other side. Rather a comic-opera effect.

"Speakers look from time to time towards the six White secretaries (heads of the departments which administer the Bantustans' responsibilities) in mute appeal for instructions. The secretaries, themselves, with expressions of slightly bemused anxiety on their faces, remind one of parents whose children are performing in a school play. You can almost read their thoughts — 'I hope he doesn't fluff it.'

"Sometimes one of the secretaries scrawls a note to be carried to the rostrum or to a speaker. The two messengers (in blue uniforms with silver buttons) run themselves ragged."[1]

The various bantustan assemblies have received little legislative or administrative power. As Mr. M. C. Botha, Minister of Bantu Administration and Development, told the Lebowa Legislative Assembly at the official opening:

"Politicians should therefore bear in mind that they should not try to take part in the administration of their territory."[2]

On matters of any importance, the Legislative Assemblies are apparently irrelevant. When KwaZulu got into debt to the tune of R22m. (£12.6m.) it became apparent that the officials had assumed powers of appropriation and expenditure which on paper belonged solely to the Legislative Assembly; the white "seconded" officials from the South African government were directly implicated, with some R9.4m. (£5.4m.) spent recklessly and without authority from the Assembly. The auditor's report stated that from the financial year 1972/73 to 1977/78, with the exception of only one year, "vast amounts were expended totally disregarding and circumventing the Legislative Assembly's control and prerogative."[3] More than R11m. (£6.3m.) was unaccounted for.[4] The irrelevance of the Legislative Assemblies in terms of budgeting and planning is underlined by the incident in the Ciskei where in 1978 the Legislative Assembly was dissolved without having considered budget estimates, unlike the regular debate at the beginning of each of the previous four years.[5] This apparently made no difference whatever to the actual administration.

Table 7 — Bantustan Politics

Bantustan	Chief Minister	Capital	Number in Legislative Assembly	Number elected	Number of chiefs or nominees	Proportion of elected members in Assembly
Bophutha-Tswana	Chief Lucas M. Mangope	Mmabatho	96	48	48	50%
Ciskei	Chief Lennox Sebe	Zwelitsha[1]	50	20	30	40%
Gazankulu	Prof. Hudson W. E. Ntsanwisi	Giyani	68	26	42	38%
KaNgwane	Chief Mokoloshi Dhlamini or Mr. Enos Mabuza[2]	Louisville	36	0	36	0%
KwaZulu	Chief Gatsha Buthelezi	Ulundi	125	55	70	44%
Lebowa	Chief Cedric Phatudi	Lebowakgomo	100	40	60	40%
Ndebele (KwaNdebele)	Chief Klaas M. Mahlangu	Katlehong	5	0	5	0%
QwaQwa	Chief T. K. Mopeli	Phuthaditjhaba	60	20	40	33%
Transkei	Chief Kaiser Matanzima	Umtata	150	75	75	50%
Venda	Chief Patrick Mphephu	Sibasa	84	42	42	50%

NB: Names of the bantustans, their capitals and other things are in constant flux; this table is based on the nomenclature as of mid-1979.

[1] To be moved to Alice.

[2] In dispute in the South African courts.

The arrogant approach of white South African officials was the subject of open conflict in Lebowa, where the Legislative Assembly appointed a commission of inquiry into the employment and ranking of civil servants, and the personal relations between white and African officials. The inquiry had to be watered down when Mr. M. C. Botha warned that the Assembly was not competent to investigate the terms of employment of its white staff, and warned the white officials not to co-operate. Interviews went ahead, however, with 532 African civil servants, and it was found that nineteen had been assaulted by white officials; 124 said they had had "serious quarrels" with them; 231 out of 759 resignations were due to "ill-treatment by whites;" three-quarters of those interviewed said that Europeans were not preparing Africans to take over their jobs, and three-quarters had received no training while in the service. There were complaints that the European agricultural overseers used Lebowa government vehicles, land and even labour for their personal farming operations. Several of them had no training or expertise of any value to Lebowa. Particular criticism was levelled at the Secretary of the Lebowa Public Service Commission.[6] The white Secretaries of the various departments were also accused of concealing information from their nominal Ministers.[7] The dispute continues to simmer without any solution being found, with Chief Minister Phatudi appealing plaintively to his officials to "mix in other matters like eating and drinking tea under the same roof"[8] and continued complaints from the Lebowa Public Servants' Association of Lebowa being run by "redundant white second-hand officials".[9] The prevalence of this problem in the bantustans is also indicated by the well-meaning attempts of James Skinner to get rid of incompetent or disloyal white South Africans from the Transkei administration which backfired so drastically—as already described in Chapter 3.

In those bantustans not classified as "independent", much of the power rests in the hands of the white South African Commissioner-General. His role is played down by the South African government, but various incidents have indicated that it is virtually unchallengeable. During negotiations for the Swazi bantustan in 1977, for example, the Commissioner-General of the Swazis presented the aspiring Goverment members with a document to sign, giving him extensive powers over all administrative functions formally transferred to the bantustan, particularly the power to move Swazis around regardless of their traditional location.[10] In KwaZulu, angry criticism of the activities of the Commissioner-General there, Mr. P. H. Torlage, were silenced in the Legislative Assembly by invoking the provisions of the constitution, rule 44 of which states that the conduct of the State President of South Africa, the Commissioner-General, or various others should not be criticised.[11] One of the Legislative Assembly members complained of "how this House has suffered from his interference and how he, in co-operation with representatives of the Central government, has made it difficult for the KwaZulu Assembly to carry out its duties over the years." However, a resolution calling on Pretoria to withdraw Mr. Torlage was prevented by cutting short the debate.[12] A similar incident occurred in Ciskei, where members of the Assembly criticised their Commissioner-General, Mr. J. Engelbrecht. He reminded them that no member could use the name of the Commissioner-General to influence the Assembly, nor address the Commissioner-General in certain circumstances, nor reflect on his conduct.[13]

The pay and conditions of the white South Africans running the bantustans reflects their superior status. Elaborate headquarters are built for the Commissioner-General in each bantustan, even while facilities for the government are at best rudimentary.[14] On independence, large sums are spent on houses and other perks for the white "advisers" newly seconded from the South African government, as observed in BophuthaTswana.[15] Salaries for the whites often exceed those of the "President" or "Prime Minister" they are supposedly serving; a white judge seconded to the BophuthaTswana government, for example, was reported to be getting a salary of R22,000 (£12,560) a year.[16] Apartheid dominates here as in the rest of South Africa. In the new capital built for KwaZulu at Ulundi the South Africans have established a "black" township with white officials living 25 miles away in a quarter of their own.[17] Conditions are so good for the whites that the top positions are used to reward the party faithful; appointments to vacant posts as Commissioner-General, particularly that of Venda, prompted even the pro-government press to describe these jobs as "political parking places" for retired Nationalist politicians.[18]

The authority given to the bantustan Ministers is strictly limited, and generally subject to veto by the South African government or its agents; the same applies to South African-appointed chiefs, headmen and petty officials all down the line. There are, however, certain activities which are of limited importance in terms of overall bantustan administration, but which impinge directly on the daily lives of the people living there: pensions and other payments, health services, and education—together with the personal enrichment of the people in charge of these. Perhaps the most enthusiastically promoted issue in the Assemblies is that of the provision of extravagant salaries and fringe benefits like luxury housing for bantustan functionaries. A major preoccupation has been in raising their own incomes from what KwaZulu Chief Minister Buthelezi called "kaffir salaries".[19] Several of them succeeded in getting increases, which led to demands from the smaller bantustans for parity with the larger ones because, as the Chief Minister of Gazankulu put it, "all the homelands do the same type of job and the money comes from the South African government."[20] Some of the chiefs are also receiving luxury housing: the KwaZulu Assembly decided to build a R250,000 (£143,000) State and guest house complex for the King of the Zulus, and the Buthelezi "tribe" is to build a R75,000 (£43,000) official residence for the Chief Minister, using a loan from the Bantu Investment Corporation which is supposedly an agency for "development".[21] The BaPhokeng tribe in BophuthaTswana, which receives royalty payments from the Impala Platinum Mine, is building a R250,000 (£143,000) mansion in the local village for their chief, complete with closed-circuit television.[22] The *Star* commented on the expenditure on prestige items:

"Cosmetic thinking is often at the heart of South African wish-fantasy. If you dress up the surface of things enough the rotten undersurface may go away. Invest some rural backwater with the dignity of a parliament and a flag and you may solve 'the Bantu problem'."[23]

The "rotten undersurface" includes considerable corruption, demoralisation and drunkenness among the chiefs and the civil service of the bantustans. A local observer has said of the Transkei officials:

"They are slack, they are happy feathering their nests and receiving bribes. They take money from pensioners and those receiving disability grants.

"They are happy to be drunk from the bottom almost to the top of the civil service."[24]

Among teachers, who work in intolerable conditions with enormous classes and no facilities, alchoholism has become so bad that it is known in the bantustans as "teachers' disease." Drinking in the KwaZulu Department of Justice has reached a "critical" level, and despite stern warnings officials in a magistrate's court were found to be drunk. The Executive Councillor for Justice, Mr. Walter Kanye, has said that excessive drinking during working hours invariably led to a shortage of revenue receipts.[25] There have been allegations that fraud, forgery and heavy drinking are widespread in the KwaZulu government service.[26]

Similar allegations have been made about local chiefs. One chief in Bophutha-Tswana, Chief Tsojoa, caused fierce faction fighting by his corruption, which included irregularities in title deeds to land.[27] Tsojoa defended himself by alleging even worse abuses by another local chief, Chief Solomon Lion, whom he described as "a jackal" taxing people and pocketing the proceeds.[28] In KwaZulu, it was reported that chiefs were demanding money from people, sometimes with threats of taking away people's cattle registration, for an elaborate wedding which was taking place.[29]

The victims of these practices are people facing total destitution if they cannot get land, cattle registration, tiny pensions and other things. In one part of BophuthaTswana, people were subject to racketeering in water because the tribal council, responsible for maintaining their own boreholes, never bothered to carry out their duties.[30] Being paid by the South Africans, and not answerable to their people as under the traditional system, these petty authorities had no incentive to provide the services they were in theory expected to. The story over pensions is the same. An opposition member of the Transkei Legislative Assembly pointed out that "many old and sickly people in the Transkei receive no benefits. Sometimes old people will tell you they did not have the money to bribe the officials who decide their eligibility for a pension."[31] A visitor to Kwa-Zulu pointed out that pensions were paid out in places far distant from where pensioners lived; people from the Msinga reserve had to travel 20km, and there is no guarantee that if they go the money will be paid. Officials can arbitrarily refuse to pay at any time, and frequently do so on the pretext that the old people have no birth certificate. There was no registration of births at the time they were born.[32] Throughout KwaZulu pensioners have been turned away from collection points.[33] In BophuthaTswana at least 1,000 pensioners, entitled to old age and disability payments on which they depended for their food, found that the independence of the bantustan resulted in their pensions not being paid. A reporter found them after they had waited four successive days for nothing; no adequate explanation was available, and they were far from their homes. One, Mrs. Celia Msiza, said that God had grown silent but she was still praying.[34] Unlike whites, Africans claiming an old age pension have to be totally destitute; at the best of times, according to one South African member of parliament, it is impossible to live on the pension given to Africans.[35]

In the field of health, standards have fallen badly as missionary organisations are forced out of the bantustans in the name of transferring control to the bantustan authorities—although the latter have been reluctant to take on the onerous task of running hospitals, and in several cases they have been run directly from Pretoria.[36] It has long been generally recognised that the South African government was hostile to the mission hospitals, clinics and other services; a Broederbond circular published recently, dating from 1975, sheds light on the issue:

"Almost 40 per cent of the white personnel at these hospitals are recruited overseas. Because of their background and political views some of them are often hostile towards State policy, sometimes in a very subtle way."[37]

Turnover in staff has become very high. One of the recent departures was of Dr. Rod McDade, medical superintendent of Mt. Coke Hospital in the Ciskei, who was summarily dismissed by the Ciskei government and told not to set foot in the building, where he had worked for four years.[38] Not all the replacements are very suitable for an African area; the medical superintendent of the all-white hospital in Umtata, for example, refused to admit an injured African baby for whom there were no facilities in the overcrowded black hospital, despite a personal request from the Transkei Minister of Health. The doctor, Dr. Hofmeyr, refused the request on the grounds that his hospital was for white only and that it was under the jurisdiction of the South African Secretary for Health in Pretoria, not the "independent" Transkei government.[39] He was expelled from the Transkei, but compensated by the South African government with a total of R167,493 (£95,640) under the pretext of buying his luxury house in Umtata; he was paid five times the municipal value of the house.[40]

Together with the elimination of experienced and often very dedicated medical missionaries, the hospitals suffer badly from being brought under the financial auspices of bantustan authorities. KwaZulu has been particularly badly hit, partly because of the presence until recently of a number of mission hospitals and partly because of the arbitrary budget cuts by Pretoria of 7% on all hospitals under KwaZulu control in 1978 as compared to the previous year (more in real terms). At this time KwaZulu had taken over 15 former state and mission hospitals and another ten were to be added to the list. The Minister of Health and Welfare, Dr. Dennis Madide, announced that some services would have to be reduced:

"My department and the hospitals and institutions under its control will make every effort to maintain services at their present level, but it must be understood that this will be an extremely difficult if not impossible task. The moral is: try not to be sick in this financial year."[41]

This was hardly a helpful statement to the increasing number of people, especially children, suffering from malnutrition and other poverty-induced diseases such as tuberculosis, typhoid fever and dysentery. A report on Natal's major black hospitals—which include the ones in KwaZulu—indicated that nearly half of the children admitted between 1960 and 1975 had been "seriously malnourished"; the incidence of malnutrition had shot up in the 1970's as a result of increasing poverty and destitution.[42]

Faced with the desperate need in the bantustans for medical care, some attempts have been made by voluntary organisations to provide some basic services. The Black Community Programme (BCP), for example, established a clinic and related services at Zinyoka, Ciskei, in 1975, together with some outstations. Free milk and the protein supplement Pronutro were provided, together with maternity services, pediatrics and general health care. It was very popular in the local community because it provided a high standard of service with two doctors, several nurses and midwives, a social worker and ambulances; however, it suffered intense hostility from the Ciskei government which refused to co-operate with it. A makeshift official clinic was put up near the BCP one, with very poor facilities; people did not attend that one. In the second year of operation there was continual harrassment of the personnel, including the arrest and detention of the two doctors and the social worker.[43] All BCP programmes were closed down in October 1977 as part of the general clamp-down in South Africa of the Black Consciousness organisations and black opponents generally. No voluntary assistance is now being accepted, it would seem; even the respectable South African Red Cross had its offer of aid to the refugees from Transkei turned down by the Ciskei Government despite the desperate conditions in the camps already described in Chapter 6.[44]

While health services are being allowed to deteriorate, some of the welfare programmes that alleviated a little the extremes of malnutrition are also being eliminated from the bantustans. In many cases there were supplementary feeding schemes for small children at risk, immunization programmes and other schemes attached to the mission hospitals, all of which have disappeared. School feeding programmes have been eliminated from KwaZulu, leading to protest from the Archdeacon of the Anglican Mission there:

"School feeding in African schools cost the country little in terms of money and much in terms of human lives. I buried five children within a few days recently, all because they did not have enough food to eat."[45]

A related programme in some areas has been distribution of milk to children. When the Durban township of KwaMashu was incorporated into the KwaZulu bantustan, the distribution of milk to creches and nursery schools run by the KwaMashu Zamokuhle Women's Welfare Society was halted for lack of money. The Port Natal Bantu Administration Board simply removed the subsidy as soon as KwaZulu took over formal responsibility.[46] This rather detracted from Chief Buthelezi's description of the transfer as "an occasion of jubilation" and his claim that "there is nothing we will not do to make the misery of our people more bearable".[47]

Perhaps the most worrying development is the contamination of water supplies, which contribute substantially to the toll of death and disease in the bantustans. As already noted, the authorities charged with maintaining water points frequently ignore their responsibility leaving people open to exploitation by local white farmers with their own boreholes, who sell water to traders who in turn charge people in the more densely populated areas enormous sums for it. In one such case, in BophuthaTswana, a reporter went to look at the source of the water selling at 60c (34p) a drum ("It's good business. There is a great demand for water. Good business," according to the trader). It turned out that the water tank was a serious health hazard with greenish slime on the bottom and rubbish and floating debris. He asked one of the traders whether the water made people ill. "Well, what can they do?" was the answer. "Just what can they do?"[48] The Natal medical survey already mentioned singled out contaminated water supplies, together with inadequate sanitation, as the major source of some of the most serious diseases, including gastroenteritis (which often kills small children), typhoid fever and dysentery.[49]

A State of Emergency

Given the enormous discrepancies between the bantustan Ministers, enriching themselves from their participation in the programme, and their increasingly poverty-stricken people, there is naturally an enormous amount of opposition—some of it outlined in Chapter 5. It is convenient for the South African government to make their bantustan appointees responsible for the repression of any opposition there, and all bantustan governments have been offered the option of adopting repressive legislation and policies along the lines of those already developed in Pretoria—subject to final authorisation by the South African government. The Minister of Bantu Administration, Mr. M. C. Botha, said at the time the enabling legislation for this was passed in 1974 that he had received requests from certain bantustan Ministers for repressive powers, including banning of individuals and their publications, prohibition of parties or organisations, and banishment to remote areas, and that he had consulted all the Chief Ministers on this.[50]

BophuthaTswana

Various measures have now been adopted by the various Legislative Assemblies along the lines proposed by Mr. Botha, and they have played a key role in the political life of the bantustans. In BophuthaTswana, for example, an amendment to the constitution was made in April 1975 to enable Chief Minister Mangope to dismiss a Cabinet Minister if he wished,[51] in line with his own personal ambitions; Mangope had earlier boasted that "our party will remain in power for ever."[52] The change was followed by the dismissal of four Ministers, including two long-standing rivals of Mangope.[53] Various other new powers were used to remove non-Tswanas who did not support him from various parts of the bantustan, and in 1974 Mangope made his official vehicles available to the South African authorities for the removal of "South Sothos" from Thaba 'Nchu, defending this by arguing the necessity of keeping out "these people who live like animals."[54]

Disputes arose during 1974 within Mangope's BophuthaTswana National Party (BNP). A group of party members introduced into the Assembly a vote of no confidence in Chief Mangope, and three reasons were cited for this: Mangope's interference in the affairs of the Madikwe regional authority by attempting to get rid of Chief Maseloane, the leader of the BNP at the time of the election; Mangope's approach to the Commissioner-General asking for the removal from the Cabinet of Chief Maseloane, claiming that the rest of the Cabinet supported this request although the Cabinet had never in fact discussed it; and the establishment of a BophuthaTswana Development Fund, of which the deed of trust had been entered in his own private capacity and all the trustees appointed by him personally, while no information was available about the source or amount of money collected. After considerable conflict, Mangope resigned from the BNP and founded a new Democratic Party, while remaining Chief Minister.[55]

As already outlined in Chapter 3, BophuthaTswana's independence was the subject of fierce opposition from many people inside the bantustan. As a result, the South African government passed a special security proclamation, No. R174 of 1977, just before the pre-independence elections. This prohibited all meetings of more than five people unless specifically authorised by the authorities; allowed for restrictions on movement and the confiscation of vehicles; and allowed chiefs and headmen to impose penalties on people not attending any of their meetings. In addition, the proclamation allowed bantustan police to arrest and detain people "until satisfied that such person has replied fully and correctly to all questions put to him;" such people are not allowed access to a lawyer. The provisions are similar to those of the South African Terrorism Act. Those administering them also tend to be the same people; for example, the head of the Mafeking Security Police was seconded to the Security Branch of the Bophutha-Tswana police force in the month before the proclamation was published.[56]

The election took place in 1977 under the shadow of the new emergency proclamation, and with half the legislature already nominated by Mangope and his party. Since four of the ruling party's candidates were unopposed, the result of the election itself was a foregone conclusion.[57] Only one-eighth of the eligible voters went to the polls, and some of these may have been forced—there were reports of forced voting and forcible registration.[58] An opposition candidate denounced the election under the emergency as "not only a farce but . . . also heavily loaded against the opposition." He alleged "certain discrepancies" before, during and after the election which included registration of voters being in the hands of the ruling party; the banning of "99 cases out of a hundred" of proposed election meetings by the opposition; three weeks taken to count the small number of votes, without the opposition being represented at the count; and more votes than there were nominees when nominated chiefs had to declare their party allegiance.[59] Not surprisingly, Mangope's party won a resounding victory.

Coercion and intimidation continued, however. An indication of the pressure applied to make people participate in the independence celebrations was the case of one school principal who received an official circular instructing teachers to participate in a music competition for independence. She and her whole staff refused: "We could not see why we should take part in a celebration we did not recognise." She was warned of the consequences of refusing to prepare for independence would be very unpleasant, and was soon afterwards dismissed.[60] There were many arrests of the opponents of independence just before the ceremony, some of the people being held under the Terrorism Act. [61] Among the students arrested during anti-independence demonstrations, it was clear that statements had been extracted from them by extreme coercion inside the prisons; the South African magistrate in the case of the stoning of Chief Mangope's car ruled that a statement signed by a 17-year-old boy was "not made freely" and was therefore not admissable as evidence; he also rejected all other statements allegedly made by the students.[62] At least two people have died in custody in BophuthaTswana, a father and son who suffocated in the back of a sealed van left in blazing heat.[63] There is no sign of any improvement in the repressive climate of the bantustan: a former Cabinet Minister, Chief James Toto, who was sacked by Mangope for his opposition to independence, has been detained for 36 days under the security laws under very harsh conditions, and continually harrassed by Mangope's security police. Interrogation focused particularly on a trip to Britain when he spoke against bantustan independence.[64] A Human Rights Congress set up in BophuthaTswana was also harrassed and interrogated by the security police and by the BophuthaTswana Minister of Law and Order; 34 men, women and children attending a meeting of the Human Rights Congress were arrested, and 19 of these claimed assault by the police. Various counter-charges were brought against the Congress leaders of alleged arson and sabotage; seven of the leaders in question later fled abroad.[65] Shortly afterwards, two journalists and a driver from *The Post*, the African paper which succeeded the banned *World* in investigating conditions in BophuthaTswana, were detained under the pre-independence emergency regulations.[66]

Ciskei

The situation in the Ciskei is similar in many ways to that in BophuthaTswana. In 1977 Ciskei too was given far-reaching powers to control political activities and detain people without trial, in Proclamation R252. The Minister of Justice can, with Cabinet approval, order police to arrest and detain people for up to 90 days if he suspects that they will embarrass the government or any person in authority, among other things. Recourse to the courts is specifically ruled out by the proclamation, which removes their power to interdict, delay or suspend any decision taken by the Ciskei government. Penalties of up to R600 or three years in prison can be imposed for "subversive or intimidating statements or actions", organising or taking part in a boycott, treating a chief or headman with "disrespect, contempt or ridicule" and failing to render services to them as required.[67] One of the opposition leaders, Mr. L. S. Mtoba, complained, "the Proclamation has a tremendous bearing on the electorate and as long as it exists, there can never be fair elections." There had already been great rancour at the conduct of elections in 1973, when the opposition had taken allegations of corrupt election practices to Grahamstown Supreme Court.[68] For the 1978 election there was a general apathy, due to the previous experience, the state of emergency and the fact that opposition candidates were not allowed to hold meetings.[69] In one incident in New Brighton, a group of women at a meeting was forcibly dispersed, including Mrs. N. Jantjies who had only just been released from detention.[70] So many detentions took place immediately before the election, involving the candidates as well as their supporters, that the three opposition parties made a joint appeal: "We call upon the Ciskei Government to release all candidates and the organisers now in detention." They also urged that the election be postponed because it was on the anniversary of the Soweto riots and the massacres of children there.[71]

The election went ahead regardless, and resulted in a landslide for the ruling party under Chief Lennox Sebe, which won every seat.[72] Immediately afterwards, reports of corrupt practices came through. Many voters complained of being instructed by polling officers, many of them openly associated with the ruling party, to show their ballot papers after marking them.[73] Others complained of official promises of help if they voted for Sebe; a family of 14 which had done so complained they had been tricked: "We were told that if we vote for party candidates we could get houses and be given all our rights."[74] Two of the opposition leaders announced that they had grounds for legal action, and alleged intimidation of voters, interference with opposition campaign meetings, refusal of registration for some opposition supporters, unfairness in the distribution of ballot papers to favour areas where the ruling party had support, and a "glaring anomaly", the absence of any copy of the voter's roll at the magistrates' offices.[75] One of the most extreme cases was in fact taken successfully to court, with the result that a former acting Chief Minister, Mr. Ntsali Mkrola, was found in the Grahamstown Supreme Court to have conducted an election with corrupt practices, undue influences and illegal practices. Mkrola was found to have been threatening to withhold pensioners' allowances and also threatening to withhold grazing rights unless people voted for him; at the polls his supporters had broken the secrecy of the poll by asking people who they had voted for.[76]

Since the elections many people who supported the opposition have been detained under the emergency proclamation. About 24 people were detained up to the beginning of 1979, including a 76 year old Methodist lay preacher.[77] Several more have gone into hiding or left the Ciskei to avoid detention, although in the case of one man who was prominent in the opposition, it was his wife who was harrassed instead, and his son and servant detained.[78] Two lawyers have also been affected, one of them detained while defending two people banished from the Ciskei under the emergency regulations,[79] and the other warned not to enter the bantustan for a court appearance to defend two men on a charge of insulting a chief; he was told that steps had been taken to detain him.[80]

As in BophuthaTswana, pressures were placed on people employed by the government to support the ruling party. Again the case which came to light was that of a teacher, Ms. Nondwangu, who reported that her principal had asked her to buy a party card and attend its rallies. "I told him that according to the regulations, teachers were not to take part in politics. I refused to buy the card and to attend the rallies." He replied that as a civil servant she had to support the government; she was then sacked, and told she must apologise to the Ciskei government before being re-employed.[81] Another hazard for those not co-operating with the Ciskei government is the "Green Berets", a group of thugs who have attacked a number of people and beaten them up with their knobkieries; they have also imposed a strict 7 p.m. curfew in Zwelitsha, the capital, although not under any recognised authority. In their most concerted action they attacked students in the streets and in boys' and girls' hostels, breaking the jaw of one boy; the action is thought to have been retaliation for attacks on the cars of Sebe's family and his Ministers. The Green Berets were seen to have arrived in official Ciskei government cars, one of them driven by Sebe's brother.[82] Sebe denied that they had any connection with his government, but said they would probably be turned into a "home guard" after training by the South African police.[83]

Chief Sebe's personal ambitions are also quite remarkable; one opponent characterised him as a "trigger happy leader", and complained, "Chief Sebe's manoeuvres make me very doubtful for the Ciskei's future. His fear of competition is at the expense of development and the Ciskei as a whole."[84]

Gazankulu

The policy of giving Chief Ministers immense personal powers has also been extended to Chief Minister Hudson Ntsanwisi of Gazankulu, who was given the power of appointing and dismissing cabinet ministers without having to seek approval for each sacking from the South African Minister of Bantu Administration. Dr. Ntsanwisi said the move would do away with the previous devious procedure, and "expedite the administration of homeland affairs."[85] The Cabinet was duly reshuffled by him following General Elections in 1978.[86] Few details are available, probably because of the absence of any investigative newspaper in the area.

KaNgwane

KaNgwane has been the focus of considerable conflict over the post of Chief Minister. Chief Mokoloshi Dhlamini, the original Chief Executive Councillor, was voted out of office by other chiefs in 1977 after refusing to sign a resolution given to him by the Commissioner-General to effect the removal of people for land consolidation purposes. This followed a meeting with the others called by the Chief Bantu Affairs Commissioner. Dhlamini took the case to the South African Supreme Court, which found that the Territorial Assembly had in fact acted unlawfully; the finding was directed also at Mr. Botha, Minister of Bantu Administration, as the person primarily responsible.[87] Meanwhile, however, the new head of the bantustan, Mr. Enos Mabuza, had signed the controversial land deal and also complied with demands to standardise all the bantustans as "self-governing" entities. According to the Supreme Court decision, the land agreement was declared null and void. However, with Chief Dhlamini back in power Mr. Mabuza took the case to the Appellate division in Bloemfontein. In terms of the rules of the Supreme Court, Dhlamini was forced to leave office a second time in favour of Mabuza. Dhlamini may appeal against the appeal.[88]

KwaZulu

In part of KwaZulu a state of emergency has existed since 1973, when the South African police were given special powers of arrest and detention for 90 days without court intervention, following a request to this effect from the Kwa-Zulu Government.[89] They were initially applied to an area of faction fighting, but Chief Buthelezi said in 1974 that he wanted the area of operation extended.[90] There have been continuous moves by the Assembly in KwaZulu to increase the power of chiefs to prohibit meetings and various other activities, as well as disciplinary measures against "negligent" chiefs.[91] This rather undermines Buthelezi's previous claim to support a "bill of rights" for the bantustan.[92]

A serious challenge to Chief Buthelezi's style of personal authority was made by the former Executive Councillor for Community Affairs, the late Mr. Barney Dladla. He was an advocate of trade unions for Africans, and while in the Kwa-Zulu Cabinet was very active as an intermediary between strikers in Natal and their employers. In March 1973 for example he threatened Alusaf that the Kwa-Zulu authorities would cut off its labour supply for the giant aluminium smelter in Richards Bay, where over 500 African workers were on strike for higher wages. As he put it:

> "This is now a challenge to prove whether KwaZulu is a government or not. If these people are employed by this firm without my approval, it would be clear that we are not a government at all."[93]

Dladla seems to have been popular as a result of his defence of workers' interests, and this was at least partly responsible for Buthelezi's move against him since the people he was working with, mainly those in white areas, were also opposed to Buthelezi and his policies.[94] Dladla charged that Buthelezi was a dictator who did not communicate with his people, and that he was deceiving overseas investors by saying that South Africa's labour situation was stable and therefore an attractive investment opportunity.[95] Buthelezi retaliated by saying that it was illegal for Dladla to criticise him, and after a fierce confrontation Dladla was first demoted to Minister of Justice, well away from his constituency of workers, and then dismissed outright in August 1974.[96] Dladla commented on the dismissal decision by the Legislative Assembly:

"Most of the members are chiefs and they dare not get out of line. My hanging on for so long was to show the outside world what separate development is all about."[97]

At the elections held in 1978, Buthelezi's Inkatha party won all the elected seats, many of them unopposed, since two previous opposition parties had by then been dissolved.[98] However, opposition was evident in the fact that only 14% of the 5 million people classified as Zulus had registered as voters and of these the percentage voting was only 37.7%, attributed to a boycott campaign by opponents[99] Buthelezi reacted angrily to allegations of intimidation and malpractice by Inkatha; as he told Dr. Connie Mulder on a visit to Ulundi: "We played your game according to the rules of the game."[100]

Considerable pressure has been placed on people to work for the Inkatha party; all teachers, for example, are "advised" to join, according to Mr. G. L. Steyn, the South African who is Secretary of the Department of Education in KwaZulu.[101] An Inkatha youth brigade has been formed, and Buthelezi told the Legislative Assembly: "Circuit inspectors were instructed to allow principals of schools to make it possible for the youth brigade to hold their meetings." Any principals or teachers who failed to carry out these instructions were "guilty of insubordination", and would be sacked.[102] Buthelezi has also said that he would suggest to the KwaZulu Public Service Commission that it take into account a civil servant's standing in Inkatha, when considering him or her for promotion. He was replying to a supporter who had asked him to ensure that everyone in key governement positions was a genuine and enthusiastic supporter of Inkatha.[103] Faced with opposition from students and others, he also called for the establishment of "vigilante groups", and he warned protestors, especially students, of a "backlash" against them.[104]

Lebowa

In Lebowa a serious move was made in March 1974 to exercise the functions of the official opposition in the Legislative Assembly, with Chief Matlala moving a vote of no confidence in the administration of Chief Minister Cedric Phatudi. Phatudi reacted by proposing to the Assembly that recognition of Matlala's role as leader of the opposition be withdrawn, and with it his annual allowance of R600. A few days later the remaining members of Matlala's party disbanded it and joined Phatudi; the assembly as a whole then voted to divide it into an Upper House, for the government nominees only, and a Lower House for the elected representatives—a move to remove the South African-appointed chiefs from their dominant position in the Assembly. It was vetoed outright by the South African Government.[105]

The new powers given to Chief Ministers to sack Cabinet Ministers were used by Phatudi to expel Mr. Collins Ramusi, a popular Minister of the Interior and Economic Affairs. The Cabinet was not consulted.[106] Ramusi had been behind some of the more intelligent positions taken by Phatudi, who complained later that the South African Bureau of State Security (BOSS) had told Lebowa chiefs and Assembly members that he and the South Africans no longer wanted Ramusi, and that he had been "tricked" into signing a document calling for Ramusi's dismissal.[107]

During the elections of 1978 a representative of one faction complained of threats to force old-age pensioners to take part in the elections or "forfeit their remunerations."[108] The chiefs, too, came under intense pressure to support Phatudi; one opponent alleged that the Minister of Works had warned chiefs that "unless they supported Dr. Phatudi all tribal applications for assistance directed to the local magistrate or the Government will not be attended to."[109] Those who fall out of favour are liable to harsh treatment; a school principal and former Chairman of a Regional Authority, Mr. Samuel Mahlangu, was dragged from his home and bundled into a car by his successors, and kept overnight in a "tribal jail" in sordid surroundings. The next day he was again taken from his home, this time by two white policemen who took him to the tribal office and handed him over to the people there with the instruction "Let them do as they please with you."[110] This incident may well be connected with the legal action taken in 1975 by Mr. Mahlangu and others, obtaining a South African Supreme Court order restraining a Lebowa chief from assaulting or interfering with them; evidence had been presented of assaults and death threats on the people for their desire to secede from the Lebowa bantustan.[111]

Ndebele

The newest bantustan, Ndebele (or Kwa-Ndebele) is still at a very early stage. The people involved were allowed to leave BophuthaTswana after much conflict there, and the central group of them are thankful not to have to move again; they have been in five different places within six months, constantly moved on from each. By comparison, the complete lack of schools, water supplies, sanitation and shops seemed a minor inconvenience, at least at the beginning.[112]

QwaQwa

Another of the minor bantustans is the tiny QwaQwa, a mountainous area the equivalent of 19km. square which has been the focus of massive resettlement since 1971, its population shooting up from 21,000 then to over 200,000 in 1978.[113] The original Chief Minister was Chief Wessels Mota; during campaigning for the 1975 elections his opponent, Mr. Kenneth Mopeli, complained that some white superintendents were threatening to evict people who did not vote for Mota's party. However, Mopeli and his party won 19 out of the 20 elected seats. This gave him less than one-third of the Assembly seats, the others being nominated chiefs; however, being the son of a chief himself Mopeli was able to get enough support from them to take over as Chief Minister.[114] Unfortunately, once in that office Mopeli showed all the bad habits of the other Chief Ministers in the bantustan system. The new opposition leader accused the ruling party of dishonesty and withholding information, particularly about a grandiose ski resort project to be set up with a German company, and which would have to be paid for by the people. Mopeli was alleged to be "loading people of the homelands with arrears they were made to incur."[115] Another opponent called Mopeli and his party "political opportunists" who promised heaven but gave the people hell.[116] They apparently took opportunism to the length of not bothering to turn up at the Legislative Assembly, since a special proclamation was issued by South Africa in 1978 to compel QwaQwa members to attend sessions, on pain of losing their seats (and their salaries).[117]

Transkei

The Transkei has had a longer period of existence as a bantustan than any other, and before that was an administrative unit as a native reserve. In 1895, representatives of the four western districts were brought together to participate in the management of local affairs through the Bunga, or local council. Participants were largely educated to a high level by missionaries, and there was already a substantial written culture and tradition of local newspapers and schools. The Bunga enjoyed some authority as a minor regional council; with the coming of the Nationalist government after World War II, however, these powers were stripped from it by means of the 1951 Bantu Authorities Act. This removed the elected councillors and gave powers to the chiefs, who by this time were mainly relics of the tribal past possessing only a few residual powers and ritualistic functions. For purposes of the Bantu Authorities system, the traditional chiefs were in many instances replaced by "new" chiefs produced by energetic research by the South African government.[118]

The Bunga had maintained a tradition, through its elected representatives, of aligning itself with protests in urban areas against the removal of African political rights. In April 1949, for example, the Bunga resolved: "This council deplores the government's policy of apartheid as a serious injustice."[119] The tradition of protest against white domination and the bantustan policy in particular was continued by the opposition in the Transkei, but this was dominated after 1955 by the "new" chiefs, who advocated Transkeian self-government in line with official policy. Following the nomination of new chiefs and the establishment of Bantu Authorities under the control of white officials, by 1960-1 large sections of the Pondos and Tembus were in revolt. In December 1960 a "state of emergency" was imposed, and Proclamation 400 put into effect. It suspended civil liberties and gave unlimited power to the South African army and police as well as the chiefs, and this has dominated life in the Transkei ever since by forbidding political meetings or organisations which conflict with the bantustan policy.[120]

At the time of the election in 1963 the power of the chiefs had been firmly entrenched, with police protection wherever they went. They were also allowed to use their emergency powers to further their own interests in the election.[121] Despite this the opposition gained a three-to-one victory, which was wiped out by the in-built majority of the chiefs in the Assembly, headed by Chief Matanzima. It was observed also that many more white officials were now sitting in the Bunga as advisers and observers.[122]

Chief Victor Poto, leader of the opposition, formed the Democratic Party which advocated full political rights for Africans throughout the Republic.[123] The party faced serious problems from the start. Some of its more determined members disappeared, some to prison, while others defected to the ruling party. Chief Poto was soon succeeded by Mr. Knowledge Guzana, a very able person but reported to be intimidated by the repressive atmosphere in which he was operating.[124]

In the second election, in 1968, Matanzima's Transkei National Independence Party (TNIP) made substantial gains which were hailed as a great success for South Africa's bantustan policy. The TNIP had 28 elected seats after the election compared to 15 before, although they still did not achieve a majority of the votes cast, only 44%. The TNIP had been better organised and financed, and had a number of official facilities at its disposal while the Democratic Party could not even afford full-time organisers.[125] A number of "irregularities" were alleged, some of them openly admitted by TNIP officials.[126] Many people in the Transkei, including the whites, regard such elections as a farce, since the people vote as the chief instructs them. This is made credible by the fact that there is no significant element of secrecy about the ballot.[127]

The third election in the Transkei was held in October 1973. In a manifesto issued on behalf of the TNIP, Chief Matanzima claimed that the policy of separate development, carried to its logical conclusion, would demonstrate that black and white could live together peacefully. The election campaign was reported to be quiet, some 700 police having been specially drafted there for the event. The percentage poll was reported as 42%. The Democratic Party was by this time in serious disarray, and lost 5 out of its 15 seats. The TNIP also lost seats, however, with 25 as compared to its previous 30. Of the rest, eight were won by independents and two were filled later in a by-election. Contrasting the TNIP's setback with pre-election forecasts of an increased majority of elected seats, the *Financial Gazette* commented that the source of dissatisfaction with Matanzima and his party arose:

". . . from a growing impatience with the climate of stagnation and inertia in the TNIP which has infected some of the government departments in the process . . . A further alienating influence is the suspicion of corruption in public and political affairs.

"Chief Matanzima's own policy statements are coming increasingly under fire, and the charge of opportunism is frequently heard. Matanzima's vacillating pronouncements on such politically-sensitive themes as Black Power and separate development—seemingly switching horses at whim—have done little to enhance his personal reputation."[128]

Considerable claims were made by Chief Minister Matanzima and others, prior to independence, that all South African security legislation including the notorious Proclamation 400 would be repealed. However, this was marred by Matanzima's warning to opposition deputies in 1974 that they might find themselves locked up after independence.[129] Later that year special emergency powers were given to one of the Ministers, Chief Jeremiah Moshesh, which enabled him to detain people without trial, demolish houses and remove people without notice. He was empowered to exact retribution for any statement undermining his authority, boycotting a meeting called by him, ridiculing chiefs, holding them in contempt or failing to show them proper respect.[130] At independence the provisions of Proclamation 400 and various South African security legislation including the Terrorism Act and Suppression of Communism Act were incorporated into a new measure, the Public Security Act. As *The World* commented: "If there is one bad habit the Transkei seems to have diligently learned from South Africa, it is contemptuous scorn for civil liberties."[131] The new Act provided for indefinite detention without trial, the banning of people by administrative decree, the outlawing of many African organisations and provision for the banishment of "recalcitrant" Chiefs and their subjects.[132] In addition, any person opposing the independence of the Transkei or claiming it to be part of South Africa is guilty of treason, with penalties ranging from five years' imprisonment to the death penalty. A State of Emergency can be declared by the Chief Minister at any time.[133]

This new law has been fully used since independence against opponents. The only independent African newspaper in the Transkei, *Isaziso*, was banned in 1978 and its proprietor and editor arrested. The apparent reason was publication of a letter complaining about the misuse of government vehicles.[134] The Methodist Church was banned in 1978, and one minister deported while others left as a result of the banning. The Church stands to lose buildings and other assets valued at R3.6 million (£2m) as a result.[135] Chief George Matanzima, brother of Kaiser and the Transkei's Minister of Justice at the time, claimed that "that money is ours, not theirs."[136] The immediate cause of the banning was the Methodists' refusal to recognise the Transkei's "independence". This was the largest church in the bantustan, where every fourth person is a Methodist.[137] A breakaway church has now been set up in the Transkei.

Arrest and detention of individuals has also been a constant feature of the Transkei since independence.[138] One case in 1978 concerned a school principal, Mr. Phumelele Cecil Vanda who had recently returned from studying in Britain; his mother, for whom he was the sole support, was refused any information about his whereabouts, how long he had been in detention or even whether he was still alive since he was under medical care when he was arrested.[139] One of those arrested, a member of the South Sotho group trying to escape Transkei rule in Glen Grey and Herschel, was held for six months in detention, threatened with a treason charge that carried the death sentence, and finally driven out of the Transkei by threats to kill him.[140] An even more serious case concerned five men alleged to be members of the African National Congress (ANC) and Pan Africanist Congress (PAC), liberation movements banned in South Africa but not (then) officially in the Transkei. They were interrogated for 17 days in Umtata by members of the South African Security Police, who then took them out of the Transkei.[141] Another 27 people, who were returned to the Transkei after serving 15 years on Robben Island, were banished to remote parts of the bantustan and it was alleged by one informant that they were being forced to work for local chiefs in return for just a bowl of food.[142]

On 2 November 1979 the Transkei government banned 34 organisations in the bantustan, including most organisations banned in South Africa. Some of the organisations banned were ANC, PAC, Inkatha, The South African Council of Churches and Black Consciousness organisations.

Detainees have died in detention in the Transkei, in circumstances like those so familiar in South Africa. An enquiry into the death of a former Umtata clerk at the magistrate's office was given evidence by several detainees on the use of torture, including severe beatings and placing a tube over their heads so that they could hardly breathe.[143] Another detainee, the heir to a chieftainship, died in the Umtata police station.[144] Even outside the jails, the Transkei police have few inhibitions. Mr. Cromwell Diko, a leader of the opposition, said recently that there was alarm in the bantustan at the amount of shooting done by the police, allegedly in the course of their duties, and mentioned a case where a man died mysteriously while accompanying the police.[145]

Venda

The first Venda elections were held in August 1973, with no political party formed by Chief Patrick Mphephu, the head of the previous territorial authority, but with an opposition party, the Venda Independence People's Party (VIP) formed under the leadership of Mr. Baldwin Mudau, a sociologist from Johannesburg. The VIP won 13 of the 18 seats for elected members in a 72% poll. Prior to the election, Mphephu arranged a three-day tour of a game reserve for the chiefs in the Assembly, although he denied suggestions that this contributed to his subsequent election as Chief Minister; Mr. Mudau asserted that many of the chiefs had been persuaded to support Mphephu in the course of the trip. Mphephu threatened to ban the VIP on two occasions during the election campaign, and later said that he hoped to introduce legislation to ban it.

At the beginning of 1974 Chief Mphephu launched the Venda National Party (VNP), which was to be tradition-orientated, concerned with preserving the powers and functions of the chiefs. When the Legislative Assembly began its session, during March, some of the Chief's former supporters crossed the floor to join the opposition, and this trend continued. It was reported that the VNP majority had dwindled from 26 to six, and that still more chiefs were considering changing their allegiance. After the Assembly had been in session for only eleven days Chief Mphephu announced its closure, thereby preventing others from crossing the floor.[146]

Venda has been under a state of emergency since 1977, in terms of Proclamation R276, with terms similar to those in force in the other bantustans. During the 1978 elections a number of irregularities were reported: instructions to chiefs and headmen to tell their people how to vote, or risk dismissal;[147] prohibition of all meetings except those of Mphephu's party; unfairness in the counting of votes in one area won by Mphephu's candidate; bribery; and even whippings of recalcitrant voters with a hosepipe at one polling station, by none other than Mphephu himself.[148] Astonishingly, given these abuses, Mphephu and his party again lost the election by a landslide, the VIP winning 31 of the 42 seats.[149] However, Government nominees make up half the Assembly and even before all the results were out the defeated Government candidates were being nominated to their former seats.[150] This curious practice has actually been used before by the South African government in "elections", packing the Coloured Representative Council with pro-apartheid people in order to overturn the results of an election they lost in 1969.[151]

Daily papers giving the news of the VIP's victory were banned in Venda.[152] VIP supporters who had been lobbying the chiefs for their support for a new government were then arrested, including 12 members of the newly-elected Assembly. To remove the chiefs from any other opponents, Mphephu organised a four-day visit to the Ciskei with them just before the election of the Chief Minister. The choice of location was no accident: Chief Sebe had himself taken the Ciskei chiefs on a tour of the Western Cape at a crucial moment to remove them from the victorious opposition.[153] On their return, the Assembly was opened with the curious spectacle of only two members of the winning party present; the others were in detention, or boycotting the Assembly over Mphephu's treachery.[154] Because of the detentions, together with Mphephu's power to dismiss chiefs who stepped out of line, Mphephu had no difficulty in remaining Chief Minister.

In July 1978 Mphephu's party thus lost the elections in Venda, but after carrying out widespread detentions of all opponents he remained in position with the support of South Africa. He then led Venda to "independence" in September 1979.[155]

The chiefs

In terms of South African legislation dating back to at least 1927, the Supreme Chief of all Africans in the country is the head of state, now the State President; all the African chiefs are arranged in a hierarchical structure, answerable to the white person who holds this post. He is empowered to legislate by proclamation in all African areas, subject to modification or repeal by the all-white House of Assembly. The State President may, among other things, define the areas to be inhabited by the various "tribes", determine rights to the occupation of land in the bantustans, appoint Bantu Authorities and chiefs, and make regulations governing marriages and succession, the administration of townships and settlements in the bantustans, and the control of meetings. Some aspects of these powers have been delegated to the Chief Ministers in the bantustans.[156] There have been many cases of independent chiefs and headmen who try to represent the wishes of their people being deposed in favour of relatives, or even complete strangers, who are willing to respond favourably to all instructions from the whites or the bantustan governments. One of the deposed chiefs, in KwaZulu, summed up the issue:

"They want my brother and his bunch of thugs because the whole lot of them are puppets of the South African government. They say 'ja baas' (yes, boss) to everything."[157]

The immediate cause of the sacking had been his refusal to join the KwaZulu Legislative Assembly, which he regarded as "a child of apartheid."[158]

Hector Ncokazi, an experienced observer and present leader of the opposition in the Transkei, has described the difference between the traditional and the modern functions of the chiefs:

"It is important to note the big contribution of the chiefs towards driving the people of the Transkei to the quagmire in which they find themselves today. First of all let us define what a chief is. A chief is a traditional ruler of all the African people who has inherited his (or her) position from his forefathers and by virtue of birth, rules in a tribal society. Present day chiefs are not necessarily the hereditary rulers of Africans, as was the case before the arrival of the white man in South Africa. Even of those who still have the original royal blood, most feel more responsible to the white government than to the African people. They use their power to satisfy the interests of the white man because they are now civil servants on the pay-roll of the government. They are appointed in terms of the laws made by the white man to entrench his domination of South Africa."[159]

Another opponent, Mr. S. J. J. Lesolang in BophuthaTswana, sees the manipulation of the chieftainship as the prime weapon in government hands, and sees the abolition of chiefs as essential to any progress:

"Our chiefs are working against the people they are supposed to serve. They are being used by the government to deprive us of what is rightfully ours."[160]

Or, as the Secretary for Native Affairs told the first Territorial Authority, in Transkei, dominated by the "new" chiefs appointed under the bantustan policy:

"Under the Bantu Authorities which you constitute you will be able to lead the people in a true sense. You will be able to tell them, not ask them, what to do. That is an important point."[161]

Each Legislative Assembly is dominated by these government-employed chiefs; as Table 7 indicates, they account for at least 50% of the Legislative Assembly in every bantustan, and in some they have a two-thirds majority or occupy all seats. The Ministers and Chief Ministers (or Prime Ministers or Presidents in independent bantustans) come directly out of this system, since they are voted into office by the Legislative Assembly. They can also use the repressive system, as illustrated above, to entrench their own position by eliminating opposition. Ministers are very often chiefs themselves; even if not, they are subject to the same system of constraints imposed by the South African government which allows them a little scope for making rhetorical anti-apartheid statements in return for a deep basic commitment to the system which pays them. Chief Buthelezi, Chief Minister of KwaZulu, is the most prominent of these; he makes some statements on issues. On the symbols of self-government, for example, he first declared that KwaZulu would not get its own national anthem and flag. ("Flags are meaningless." "People do not eat flags").[162] Within two months, KwaZulu had a flag.[163] On the question of foreign investment in South Africa he has a different position for every season. In November 1977 he was advocating economic sanctions against South Africa: "I honestly believe that the only way to salvage what is left of a chance for peaceful change is through the international community applying sanctions." Five months later he was back to the official government line, opposing sanctions on the grounds that blacks would suffer. It is interesting that when put to a large African crowd in Soweto, the majority of the audience showed strong opposition to this latter position.[164]

Irritation is sometimes expressed by Buthelezi's fellow Chief Ministers, who resent his image as an opponent of the system. Chief George Matanzima, then Deputy Prime Minister of Transkei, told his Legislative Assembly "to a chorus of encouragement from members of the ruling party" that Buthelezi was a political chameleon and a charlatan. While claiming to be head of Inkatha, a party with pretensions to leadership in the urban areas, he was in fact principally the Chief Minister of KwaZulu. "This chief goes around in a big black Mercedes, ZG 1, belonging to the Zulu government, not Inkatha. He goes to Pretoria as Chief Minister of KwaZulu, not head of Inkatha."[165] Buthelezi defends himself by saying he has no alternative: "Each and every one of you knows that as blacks we operate from a position of powerlessness."[166] More recently, "Although I participate in the policy of the government regardless of my reservations, I act in good faith. I don't sabotage the policy."[167] Speaking to critical students in Addis Ababa, he defended his role: "We in South Africa are not free agents, as blacks. The policies have been imposed on blacks by force."[168] Chief Matlala, the former Chief Minister of Lebowa summed up the conflict between those who had accepted the bantustan policy and those who condemned it:

"The critics often say that the government is lying and can never fulfil its promises. I do not think in these days the government can afford to lie to us and to the civilised world by making promises it cannot fulfil.

"If on the other hand the critics prove to be right, then we as homeland leaders must accept that we have allowed ourselves and our people to be sold into perpetual slavery to the White man and that we are government stooges."[169]

While travel and free debate for the chiefs within South Africa is severely limited and subject to official permission from the South African government,[170] a major benefit of the role of Chief Minister is regular travel throughout Western Europe and North America, where they are feted as "leaders", well away from the sordid details of day-to-day contact with their South African masters. They are often on these foreign trips rather than attending to the official duties inside their bantustans; Chief Mangope, for example, failed to show up for the official handing over of the new BophuthaTswana government headquarters at Mmabatho, because he had just left for a European tour;[171] Chief Minister Mopeli of QwaQwa was absent for the annual conference of his party because of an official visit to West Germany.[172]

While abroad, the Chief Ministers are taken on a round of interviews, press conferences and meetings where they alternately criticise apartheid, defend their own position in the system, and ask for foreign aid and investment for their favourite projects. They are also given special dispensation to meet with their overseas sponsors from investing countries, in sheltered locations inside South Africa itself, a favourite venue being the Holiday Inn near Johannesburg Airport where the rules against interracial mixing have been suspended by the South African government specifically with this kind of contact in mind.[173] These kinds of meetings, in South Africa and abroad, promote an image for the government of a liberalising society where real dissent by African "leaders" is possible, while at the same time promoting foreign economic involvement in the Republic.

In the process, the Chief Ministers are of course influenced by their overseas contacts, especially in the United States, and they return home to their bantustans full of new but unfortunately rather impractical ideas not relevant to the people's own expressed needs; they tend to be rejected more often than not by those involved. One example was Chief Buthelezi telling people in the United States that he and Matanzima were determined to have a federation of their bantustans, and announcing this on his return to South Africa without having consulted Matanzima at all. He had also omitted to ask Mr. M. C. Botha for permission — Botha immediately issued a statement saying that the agreement of the South African government would be needed for such a federation, and it would definitely not be forthcoming.[174] However, it is the bantustan Ministers' original statements which get all the publicity — especially from the official South African media — and not the subsequent denial, or the later action which directly contradicts the former promises. Chief Matanzima is himself particularly prone to the urge to make extravagant promises while abroad, or on his return. He returned from a visit to the United States in 1972, and in an emotional speech announced that the visit had "inspired him with a spirit of nationalism and a refusal to accept second-class citizenship."[175] He got a little carried away after another such trip in 1973, announcing Transkei independence at East London airport, a white area, without any prior consultation with people inside Transkei.

Inside the bantustans, as well as in the urban areas, there is frustration and anger at the pretensions of chiefs who are themselves living in luxury, claiming to speak for Africans without any attempt to consult with them. The Chief Ministers are seen by politically aware people to be promoting South African government policy — for example, Chief Buthelezi's role in promoting the "dialogue" policy which gave the illusion of liberalism in South Africa while the reality was increased repression. Buthelezi helped to arrange Prime Minister Vorster's visit to Liberia, for example. As he justified himself: "Nobody . . . should try to be brave on our behalf. This is dangerous, and indeed explosive."[176] He admitted, "Everyone knows that I am under fire in this country and up north among young people for believing in non-violence . . . "[177] Mangope, faced with increasing frustration among his own people, has warned, "Our young people are not going to be as patient as we are. We have repeatedly warned the Whites of this, but they ignore our warnings . . . "[178] Matanzima has conceded that he is attacked for his conservative attitude:

"Among the youths there is a movement towards Black Power. I advise the whites to reason with us. We will not grab the land we want — but our youths will take the land by force."[179]

It is interesting that a survey in 1974 in some of the bantustans showed that the majority of people there were indifferent or ignorant about their nominal "leaders". Only 8% of people in KwaZulu expressed admiration for their Chief Minister, 4% in the Transkei and 1% in Lebowa and BophuthaTswana. In the Transkei, less than one in five even knew the name of their Chief Minister.[180] However, the younger and better educated people are aware, and vociferous in their condemnation. The South African Students' Organisation (SASO) called on the chiefs to withdraw from participation in the bantustans, and denounce them, especially Buthelezi, for giving the people false hopes that apartheid can benefit them, as well as giving credibility to South African policies internationally.[181] Their interpretation is supported by no less an authority than former Prime Minister Vorster, who told Africans:

". . . if there are people who are raising your hopes that there will one day be one man one vote in the white parliament for you, then they are misleading you, for that will never happen."[182]

Divide, and rule

With the bantustans divided arbitrarily into ten different bits, each comprising scattered areas of old reserve land with continual additions and deletions and occasionally transferred from one bantustan government to another, the stage is set for continual disputes between Chief Ministers and their followers which, together with the foreign trips, take up a large amount of their time and energy. The Chief Ministers can be relied on to carry on lengthy disputes with each other over their shortest commodity — land — as well as the delicate matter of who has jurisdiction over which people. At the same time, of course, they are preoccupied by the necessity to maintain their own rather precarious position inside their own bantustan by the surveillance and repression of opposition at home, as already outlined in this chapter.

The interminable disputes among the Chief Ministers are far too complicated for adequate description here. At the time of writing, there are major fights going on between the Transkei and Ciskei over the South African government's transfer of Ciskei territory, Herschel and Glen Grey, to the Transkei just before independence; between QwaQwa and the Transkei over South Sothos in the Transkei; between Gazankulu and Lebowa over a border dispute (if the South African government does not resolve this, according to Gazankulu, "blood will flow"[183]); between the Transkei and KwaZulu over disputed territory around Umzimkulu allocated to the Transkei; between QwaQwa and BophuthaTswana over a Sotho area allocated before independence to the latter; between QwaQwa and KwaZulu over Sothos there; between Venda and Gazankulu over their border; between Ndebele and BophuthaTswana over Ndebeles in the independent bantustan; and between KwaZulu and KaNgwane over Swazis in KwaZulu. In many cases, the "tribal" label given to a community is one of convenience rather than reality; for example, in the strife-ridden area of Thaba 'Nchu, recently transferred to BophuthaTswana, the "South Sothos" of the Kromdraai squatter camp are of mixed origin; the people involved would describe themselves as of various different groups, including many Xhosas and even some Tswanas — although their removal is ostensibly in the interest of Tswana hegemony.[184]

The independence issue is perhaps the most powerful divider, and is fully exploited as such by the South African government which has rewarded those Chief Ministers who accept independence with extra pieces of land taken from the others. Attempts to build some kind of federation took place in Transkei, where it was agreed that none of the Chief Ministers would negotiate for independence without consulting the others. A request was also made to the South African Prime Minister for a joint interview.[185] The *Sunday Times* reported that Chief Matanzima had completely undercut the strategy proposed, firstly by reaching a secret agreement beforehand with Mr. Vorster about Transkei independence, and secondly by cutting down the proposed one-day session for planning a joint strategy for the meeting to two hours.[186] When it was the turn of BophuthaTswana to become independent, all the Chief Ministers either boycotted the event, or were not invited, with the exception of two (Sebe of Ciskei and Mphephu of Venda), who were moving towards independence themselves while others remain opposed.[187]

Another source of friction is the claim by KwaZulu's Chief Buthelezi and his Inkatha party to be a national "liberation movement" which represents all Africans in South Africa, and which all the bantustan governments should work with through its umbrella organisation, the South African Black Alliance (SABA), also headed by Buthelezi. It originally claimed the adherence of the Coloured Labour Party and the Indian Reform Party; since then the ruling parties in QwaQwa and KaNgwane have also joined.[188] Mopeli of QwaQwa seems to support SABA in the same way as he advocates working with the South African whites — "always enterprising" and good people to co-operate with.[189]

All the other bantustan Chief Ministers are keeping their distance, however, distrustful of what they see as Buthelezi's personal ambitions in the name of "Zulu imperialism", as was apparently agreed at a meeting in early 1979 of Chief Ministers.[190] Even in his own KwaZulu bantustan, as described, Buthelezi and his Inkatha party have failed to secure whole-hearted support from many people, although there is no longer any organised opposition. Inkatha's backbone is the KwaZulu government employees who are required to join the party in order to keep their jobs. He has undoubted support in some urban areas, mainly from Zulus, but there is also extreme opposition.

CHAPTER 8
Development?

The policy of "separate development", originally a euphemism for apartheid, has itself become somewhat tainted in the eyes of the world. In the continual search for new terminology that will make South Africa's racial policies seem consistent with international norms, however, one of the elements in "separate development" has been isolated: with the bantustans unofficially declared "underdeveloped", and with the general connotations of progress attached to the concept of "development", this word is proving a useful one in the search for international approval. Major efforts are being made to change the names of university departments to "development studies", with links to be set up with such centres elsewhere; there is a new government journal, *Development Studies in Southern Africa*, almost exclusively devoted to the bantustans together with the Corporation for Economic Development (CED), formerly the Bantu Investment Corporation, the Bureau for Economic Research re Bantu Development (Benbo) and many other such institutions. Throughout there is a solemn use of technocratic jargon, interspersed with much quantitative analysis, which is presumably intended to impress those who think development is a statistical issue rather than one of human welfare. Benbo (now Benso) has produced an impressive *Economic Revue* for each of the bantustans, filled with elaborate maps and tables, which epitomises this approach.

The idea of "developing" a number of fragments of land, which were originally set aside as reserves which would offer their inhabitants no means of living except by selling their labour outside, is a strange one. Taking into consideration the continual dumping of old, young and handicapped people into these areas, and the continuing deterioration of their subsistence agriculture base, the task would appear virtually impossible. Other factors make the idea of "development" a remote concept for the bantustans. Firstly, the important decisions are taken in Pretoria in the interests of the white minority government, as Professor Ntsanwisi, Chief Minister of Gazankulu, has pointed out. Refuting a claim by a senior South African government official that the bantustans were in charge of their development, he said this was the theory but in practice, "the powerlines go to the Department of Plural Relations and then they decide."[1] Where decisions are taken inside the bantustan Governments, it is almost invariably by the white South African officials there. Chief Sebe of the Ciskei has complained bitterly of the type of official involved, in Pretoria and in the bantustans: "You have got people there who have been involved in administration for years as Bantu Affairs

Commissioners, but they just haven't any concept of development." There were no staff capable of the detailed planning, let alone the technicians able to carry out any coherent plan.[2] The scandal of unaccounted expenditure in KwaZulu totalling R22 million in all, already mentioned in chapter 7, was attributed by the auditor to "gross negligence" on the part of the white officials. Among other actions they had bought new cars "indiscriminately" and "without the necessary care and attention." Many vehicles had been kept in an open space without being used for months, some for more than a year. In addition, there was an overall deficiency in the accounting system: "an absolute lack of internal control and efficient check measures throughout KwaZulu." Although certain offices were collecting revenue, receipts were not issued nor cash books maintained.[3]

Despite the array of statistics produced in the Benbo and other publications on the bantustans, much of the most basic information is completely lacking. The Minister of Bantu Administration has admitted that much of the reserve land has never been surveyed, and of that which is, no proper instruments were used so that "particulars to be furnished may not be accurate."[4] Population figures are also incomplete. Many questions about area, population and economic activity in the bantustans which are put in the South African House of Assembly are not answered because of these deficiencies, because "the concept of economic activity . . . is being interpreted in different ways," or because formal responsibility has been transferred to the bantustan government, and the South African Minister refuses to answer.[5]

Basic geography is also a block to any rational economic planning, with the great fragmentation of the bantustans (well over a hundred pieces for KwaZulu) and the large distances between the pieces, as well as the fact that trade and communications are inevitably linked to the local networks, all part of "white" South Africa. Many bantustan governments have no jurisdiction over posts and telegraphs, aviation, overall financial management or many other essential elements of coherent policy. For some of the bantustans, particularly Bophutha-Tswana, any attempt to travel around the whole territory would mean spending as much time outside as inside the bantustan.

The prospect of achieving economic viability depends on the bantustans obtaining considerably more land, existing economic centres and usable ports adjacent to their main areas — none of which will they get. Pretoria's attitude is well indicated by its excision of the new Richards Bay harbour from KwaZulu. The KwaZulu Legislative Assembly commented:

"If the Republican Government seriously wanted KwaZulu to be a viable state, then Richards Bay should be our port so that we have an outlet to the sea and a possibility of getting anywhere near economic viability.[6]

The same applies to the Ciskei and East London. A lengthy report on Ciskei development by the Institute of Social and Economic Research at Rhodes University concluded that the Ciskei was completely dependent on East London and other white areas near it, and could never develop independently.[7] Criticising the attempt to do this along the lines of bantustan policy, Prof. J. B. Daniel of Rhodes University pointed out the waste involved:

"All Government thinking and planning takes place within the framework of Homeland development and apartheid, and I would submit that this is an expensive process, as virtually all aspects of development have to be duplicated."[8]

Financing the bantustan economy

The low priority which is given to the bantustan policy in terms of actual expenditure is obvious in the budget of the South African government. The 1975-6 budget allotted only R385 million for the whole bantustan deal — infrastructure, education, economic development, land purchase, administration, social welfare, pensions and all other items — while the four provinces received R1,254 million, almost four times as much, in spite of the fact that they are not expected to be involved in massive new programmes such as vast population removals and the construction of what are purported to be eight "governments" complete with new capital cities and new administrations. Another R948 million was allotted to the defence budget.[9] Altogether, expenditure on bantustan items totalled only 5.9% of the national budget for 1975-6, although it covered basic services, education and health, as well as land purchases.

It has always been difficult to form an accurate picture of government expenditure on the bantustans, because of the inconsistencies in the presentation of budgets and the fact that development expenditure is confused with routine administration, payments to whites or to agencies of the South African government, and the establishment of "townships" or camps to which people taken from their homes are sent. The estimates provided in debates are also unreliable. In 1967, for example, the government announced a R490-million, five-year development plan for the bantustans, to cover the period April 1966 — March 1971. However, the plan had apparently been in operation for a year at the time of announcement, and scrutiny of the figures shows that it was merely an extract of the portion of the fiscal expenditure allocated to the reserves, and so not the supplementary "development plan" which the announcement indicated. It even included expenditure on urban areas and services there.[10]

A management consultant has reviewed the budget data for the last 15 years, and reported that the statistics are incomplete, obscure and inconsistent. Funds received by the S.A. Bantu Trust and spent by it in the bantustans are particularly hard to disentangle.[11]

In the five years 1956-61 the funds for "development" in the reserves totalled about R13.5 million, although the government had previously announced a budget of R73.2 million. This was the first indication that the Government would ignore the financial requirements of its own Tomlinson Commission, which had estimated that about R208 million would be needed for development in the first ten years.[12]

In 1961 the first "development plan" was announced for the next five years, with a total announced budget of R114,342,000. Of this, however, R75,950,000 was for "town planning", i.e. the costs of deportations and establishments of camps and townships in the bantustans to replace existing homes — a process which can hardly be classified as "development." The remaining R38 million was for a variety of projects, probably including the "rehabilitation" or "planning" policy, which results in massive shifts of people within the bantustans and also requires the replacement of existing housing and other facilities. Thus, in the first ten years after the Tomlinson Commission Report, the amount of development finance was at most only a quarter of the amount recommended.

The 1966-71 plan showed a total expenditure of R490 million, but was not comparable to the previous plans. The Minister of Bantu Affairs, Mr. Botha, did not even lay it before parliament, explaining that it was "simply a developmental working document."[13] It is not possible to relate particular items directly to the headings of the plan, but it appears that the heading "education," a major item at R163 million, included all educational facilities for Africans both in white areas and the bantustans; the amounts already voted by parliament were in fact substantially less than this at the time the plan was announced.[14] The heading "physical development," with R162 million, did not appear to relate to any specific heading in the budget, but probably covered the same items as "town planning" in the first plan, namely deportation and resettlement costs. "Social development," probably relating to pensions, rehabilitation centres, and settlements for the aged and unfit, also appeared to cover money spent on all Africans, whether in the white areas or the bantustans. R50 million for "land purchase and capital needs" probably covers the purchase of white farms for consolidation, and another R39 million for "economic development" was intended, according to a statement by Mr. Botha, primarily to encourage white-controlled industry to operate in the bantustans on an agency basis.[15] A breakdown of bantustan finance is available for the financial year 1974-5, when a total of R353,915,000 was allocated as shown in the Table on page 97.

The budget is entirely within the responsibility of the Department of Co-Operation and Development, which prepares the annual budget requests on behalf of the bantustans and the various government agencies involved in bantustan policy. It may be noted that the largest increase over the previous year in this budget was the amount allocated for land purchase, almost three times as large as the R8,525,000 in 1973-4.[16] Apart from the allocations to the bantustan governments, which cover largely the services nominally administered by them such as education and roads, major items are the purchase of white land, establishment of African townships for deportees, and the provision of share capital for government-owned corporations operating in the bantustans mainly through white investors.

The extreme dependence of the bantustans on the financial allocations of the Department of Co-operation and Development is evident from a comparison of income received from that source as compared to the revenue raised by the bantustan government, from sources such as local taxation, licence fees, fines, rents, liquor profits, etc.

Bantustan finances 1974-5

	R1,000
Payment to homeland governments	216,153
Health services and hospitalisation in the bantustans	44,097
Construction of access roads to Bantu areas	1,316
Services in the Eastern Caprivi[1]	3,749
Purchase of land	25,000
Development of Bantu areas by the S.A. Bantu Trust[2]	61,975
Compensation to whites in the Transkei	1,625

Notes: [1] This is in Namibia; proportions of the other items also presumably include Namibia.
   [2] This included the following items:

Establishment of townships	17,750
Hospital buildings	7,228
University buildings	2,508
Share capital for corporations	27,700
Other services not yet transferred to bantustan governments	12,839
Less: sums available from the S.A.B.T.'s own sources	6,050

Source: Survey of Race Relations, 1974 (Institute of Race Relations, Johannesburg, 1975), pp. 185-6.

Table 9 shows the overwhelming dependence of the bantustans on South African government finance, for the eight bantustans where figures are available. For "independent" BophuthaTswana, the Transkei and Venda, the South African financing was 82.5%, 83.7% and 83.2% respectively, and for the next bantustan on the way to "independence", the Ciskei, the dependence is 85.4%.

Another phenomenon is the trend towards much greater dependence on South African government finance between 1972-3 and 1975-6; for most of the bantustans, their share of the total financing was reduced by about a half. As more reponsibilities are transferred to the bantustan governments, an increasing proportion of their income will have to be in the form of subsidies from Pretoria. As Table 9 also indicates, government revenues are almost as high, or higher than the total gross domestic product for some of the bantustans. There are two major responses by the bantustan governments to their lack of funds. The first is to make desperate attempts to extract more money from the people there in the form of taxes. in Lebowa, for example, local taxes were raised by 500% in 1978, from R2 to R10 a year (£5.70), leading to violent protests:

"Our brothers outside are unemployed. The labour bureaux are full of people who cannot even buy half a loaf. Labourers of this very government get R40 a month. How are these people expected to cope with the increase when 85% of them still owe the R2?"[17]

Increases in taxation seem to be associated in particular with bantustan independence. In the Transkei, following unauthorised expenditure over and above the 1976-77 budget, an immediate amendment was published to the Transkei Taxation Act allowing the President to raise a special new tax of R10 a year on every-

Table 9 — **Financing the bantustans** (R1,000)

Bantustan	Gross Domestic Product[1]	Direct expenditure by SA Govt.[2]	Grants from SA State Revenue Fund[2]	Internal bantustan revenue[2]	Total revenue in the bantustan	% contribution from internal revenue 1975-6	% contribution from internal revenue 1972-3[3]
Bophutha-Tswana	150,977	17,996	38,419	11,952	68,367	17.5%	35.7%
Ciskei	45,971	19,422	25,974	7,760	53,156	14.6%	30.5%
Gazankulu	24,364	6,368	9,108	4,791	20,267	23.6%	42.2%
KwaZulu	135,399	55,482	71,996	20,590	148,068	13.9%	40.6%
Lebowa	91,094	19,356	25,605	13,338	58,299	22.9%	47.6%
QwaQwa	4,529	2,688	1,999	4,829	9,516	50.7%	26.2%
Transkei	n.a.	25,272	71,080	18,730	115,082	16.3%	32.3%
Venda	15,361	3,894	11,459	3,111	18,464	16.8%	25.5%

NB: No figures are available for KaNgwane and Ndebele.

[1] 1974 figures from the Minister of Statistics, *Debates*, 15.2.77.

[2] Figures for 1975-6 from South African Institute of Race Relations, *A Survey of Race Relations, 1977* (SAIRR, Johannesburg, 1978) p. 316.

[3] Calculated from figures in *Survey 1972, 1973* and *1974*. The figure for QwaQwa is for 1973-4.

one, plus alterations to livestock taxes.[18] In the 1977-78 budget a total of R28.8 million was to be raised from new taxes on income, huts, immovable property, a general levy and a new livestock tax. The latter in particular raised very strong criticism.[19] In BophuthaTswana, circulars were sent to all those living in the bantustan just before independence, asking the value of their property and livestock — obviously with the intention of imposing heavy taxes on these. One opponent, Chief Maseloane, protested vainly that the people, "who are almost starving to death", would be quite unable to raise the money.[20]

The attempt to raise revenue internally is a poor solution to the problem; even worse, however, is trying to get a more serious allocation from South African government to cover the budget. Chief Sebe of the Ciskei has characterised the South African approach to financing development as "niggly, pennypinching and miserly," and pointed out that the pittance provided is even smaller than contributions from the central government to the neighbouring white town of East London.[21] In KwaZulu, where a preliminary development plan commissioned from a Natal planning firm outlined a requirement of about R4,599 million (£2,626 m) in fixed capital expenditure, not even the recurrent costs of existing services can be met from the South African allocation. The effect of the cuts on health care has been outlined earlier; in addition, they meant that there would be fewer people getting pensions, fewer teachers employed, no books for the schools and some of the agricultural projects would have to be abandoned.[22] Even KwaZulu, however, is not in as serious a financial crisis as the Transkei, which had a R96 million (£54.8 m) budget deficit in 1978. The *Financial Times* commented:

"The showpiece of South Africa's policy of separate development, the Republic of Transkei, is rapidly degenerating into a tragic parody of the problems of Third World development. A combination of political autocracy and financial incompetence are leading the impoverished tribal homeland rapidly towards a financial crisis, or even into insolvency."[23]

The South African *Financial Mail* has reported that prospects for funding this deficit, 29% of total budgeted expenditure, are virtually nil. Hundreds of middlemen had come through Umtata looking for "a quick buck" but nothing had materialised. Foreign banks were refusing to have any dealings with the Transkei, the only prospect of a foreign loan being if South Africa guaranteed it — which it had so far refused to do. The local South African market was also extremely sceptical of investing any money in the bantustan although some R16 million (£9.1 m.) had been raised in South Africa the previous year.[24] It is curious that while a list of priorities for capital expenditure had been drawn up, to see which could be cut, this had been done by the civil servants — most of them seconded from South Africa — and no Transkei government Minister had seen the list although it had been out for months.[25]

The major reason for the sudden financial squeeze on several bantustans is not merely the low levels of financing available; these have stayed fairly static, and predictable, for several years. The new factor is expenditure of considerable sums on "the trappings of independence" as the *Financial Times* calls it, or prestige projects of little or no value to the mass of the people.[26] New government buildings, stadiums, airports, luxury housing for officials and Ministers, together with inflated salaries for the latter (26% of the budget in the Transkei) mean a major new drain on already limited resources.[27] QwaQwa is planning a R17,000 statue of a local chief.[28] In BophuthaTswana about R500,000 was spent by the government on an abortive attempt at publicity by promoting a boxing match. The opposition saw this as gambling away the bantustan's meagre revenue.[29] The Transkei acquired 3,000 new uniforms, costing R286,000 (£163,000) for a projected future army.[30] It has also allocated R120,000 (£68,500) for a "consulate" in Johannesburg (despite having theoretically no diplomatic relations with South Africa) and R280,000 (£160,000) for an embassy in BophuthaTswana. Border posts for some roads will cost R2 million (£1.1 m) but still leave several routes in and out without any check. About R198,000 (£113,000) has been voted for a stand at South Africa's Rand Show, and R600,000 (£343,000) for public relations offices, information centres and overseas trips by officials which are not covered by official invitations.[31] One of the most lavish parties in New York was given by the Transkei office there.[32] Some R363,000 (£207,000) disappeared with an unoffical "ambassador", Dr. Richard Blom, who was supposed to be doing a little public relations on its behalf; he was last heard of leading a Transkei mission to Chile.[33] The total amount spent on independence, and the promotion of the idea internationally, have never been calculated; however, the Ministry of Bantu Affairs reported in 1978 that its own overspending of about R18 million (£10 m) on the 1977-78 budget had been due mainly to its efforts to promote independence.[34]

The development corporations

Much of the "development" in the bantustans is outside the control of the governments and in the hands of various state corporations set up by the South African government, and wholly owned and controlled by them. Virtually all the directors are whites; although there has been some discussion about placing representatives of the Legislative Assemblies on the boards they would not be able to vote on decisions.[35]

There has been vociferous protest from the chiefs and others in the bantustans at their exclusion from both the running of the corporations and from their concessionary facilities. Chief Mangope of BophuthaTswana has said:

"Instead of becoming a dynamic catalyst for economic progress, the BIC became a monopoly, and thereby an obstruction. It assumed that we in the homelands were economically immature . . . but to assume that it can monopoleis all negotiations is to defeat its own purposes."

He made a general point about development which is familiar to many of those in the field; "People will absorb and implement change only the extent to which they take part in it."[36] On the proposed formation of a KwaZulu Development Corporation, Chief Buthelezi said that judging from previous experience it would be an instrument for the "economic neo-colonialism of blacks."[37] He has pointed out that the operations have a virtual monopoly on business sites in most of the new bantustan townships, which are to be the focus for future development and employment creation.[38] Chief Phatudi of Lebowa has objected to their monopolistic control of commercial agriculture. Other chiefs had made similar complaints, while the corporations seem also to be unpopular among all the bantustan people involved. The XDC was dubbed locally the "Xhosa Destruction Corporation" and it is alleged that its methods of attracting foreign investors perpetuate bantustan poverty instead of abolishing it, because of the low-wage policy. There is particular criticism of the mishandling of the local trading stores; services have been curtailed and many have been closed down, resulting in great hardship to the local people who must sometimes walk long distances for essential supplies.[39]

The corporations have also come under attack for mismanagement and corruption. Eleven cases of corruption within four years were reported by the Minister of Bantu Administration in 1974; in eight cases, white officials had borrowed money under African cover, and in others they had colluded with construction companies over tenders. 53 officials were dismissed.[40] A parliamentary Commission of Inquiry into the BIC was launched at the end of 1974, as allegations of further irregularities in the granting of a construction contract to Multibou, and further complaints of irregular dealings, continued to be heard.[41] Its report, however, covered up rather than exposed the details of corruption. One of the industrialists operating in a growth point managed by the BIC said, "I get what I want from them. It all depends on with whom you negotiate, and let me tell you, it is only a matter of bribery and corruption." A BIC official reportedly told the parliamentary inquiry of "an inner circle of top officials" who had enriched themselves by hundreds of thousands of Rands through certain dealings.[42] The government has refused to disclose the names of those with a conflict of interest. It has been pointed out that the full accounts of the BIC and other corporations are not available for scrutiny by the parliament or public, and there have been rumours of enormous losses in some of the concerns financed and managed by the corporations. Instances were cited of "ineffective control of the collection of money" and "weaknesses in planning and internal management as well as in interest control."[43] The solution, as is often the case, was a change of name: the Bantu Investment Corporation is now called the Corporation for Economic Development (CED).

It is dangerous for people in the bantustans to criticise the development corporations, it would seem. Dr. Ramusi, who had led the attack on the BIC for "stealing" Lebowa land near the Steelpoort River for one of its projects, was dismissed from the Cabinet immediately afterwards. He had accused the Chief Minister of "co-operating closely" with the BIC in making the bantustan "a captive of vested interests," and advocated removing it "with the same clear-cut reactions of an experienced surgeon so that future generations would have a life assured free of hunger, sickness and helplessness."[44]

The abrupt departure of Mr. James Skinner from the Transkei Development Corporation (TDC) after attempts to purge it of some of the whites at the top levels, has been outlined in Chapter 3. The same problem led to the dismissal of another outsider, Prof. Joseph Ben-Dak of Israel, who had been appointed planning adviser to the Transkei government and proceeded to try reforming the TDC. Among other things he reported to his Ministers that certain of the South African officials were incompetent; that they badly needed to employ some proper "professionals" with the relevant skills; that it was in control of operations which would be better handled by private interests or the Government; that the functioning of the corporation was totally devoid of serious commitment to national processes of planning and to the decisions of the Transkei Government; that there was serious financial misconduct bordering on the illegal; and that a complete independent evaluation of the TDC's role in the Transkei should be undertaken. Not only was Prof. Ben-Dak sacked for his pains, but so was a TDC official who had talked to him and adopted some of his recommendations, Mr. Fred Fehrsen.[45] There was a substantial loss to the Transkei resulting from the TDC mismanagement — a net loss of R864,000 (£500,000) in the first year of operation was announced after Ben-Dak's departure.[46] The Transkei government had been channelling much of its development finance through the corporation.[47]

Development Corporation projects

A large part of the corporations' resources are taken up by the transfer of trading stores, garages and other retail outlets in the bantustans to new ownership, with the corporations either running them directly, leasing them back to the former owners or leasing them to individual Africans. It is hard to see this process as development, since very few of the enterprises are concerned with production; "development" finance is used only to transfer ownership on existing ventures rather than create new ones. Compensation to the previous owners is often exorbitant, and the operations commonly decline in terms of efficiency and the quality of service offered to the local people in terms of the range and price of food and other items.[48]

One of the few journalists to visit a bantustan together with a group of South African industrialists, recorded their reaction as "one of utter astonishment" at being shown a few missionary schools and clinics taken over by the Xhosa Development Corporation but dating back 50 years; they demanded to know what the corporation had itself built. The reporter claimed that the XDC had not even got to the stage of producing a basic topographical survey of its area, Transkei and Ciskei, "let alone reached the stage of a systematic classification of mineral and other resources, spending power, availability of power, water, transport, communications and other facilities."[49]

The beneficiaries of the take-overs include a few favoured Africans, but these are in a clear minority compared to white business people and the development corporations themselves. Loans provided by the Bantu Investment Corporation

(BIC) from its formation in 1959 until 1974 were divided as follows, according to the Managing Director, Dr. Adendorff:[50]

African-owned enterprises	R14m.
Corporation-owned enterprises	R20m.
White-owned enterprises	R43m.

Africans, then, received only 18% of the finance provided by the corporation. Since some of the scandals in the BIC have involved officials getting loans for themselves under African cover, it may even be somewhat less than this. It has been pointed out that African deposits in BIC savings banks have exceeded the loans provided to Africans by a considerable margin.[51] As of 1968, only 14.3% of all African applicants received loans.[52]

The terms of loans provided to Africans are also less favourable than those for whites. White investors in the bantustans are offered loans of up to 60% of their capital investment at an interest of only 2.5% payable over 10 years, tax concessions for 50% of the employed labour force, and 10% of the value of plant and equipment. None of these incentives is offered to African investors.[53] Chief Mangope of BophuthaTswana complained of the BIC:

"I would like this corporation to render a service to us more than make a profit from us."

He pointed out that the government made aid loans to other countries at 4%, while the BIC rate for Africans was $7\frac{1}{2}$%.[54] Those who are receiving loans from the development corporations are generally of urban origin with unusually high levels of education; few of the inhabitants of the bantustans are benefitting. A study of the loans has concluded that they create a "synthetic entrepreneurship," based on the contradiction that only people already in possession of the skills are involved, but at the same time subjected to rigid controls by the corporations which run counter to the development of initiative and greater entrepreneurial skill.[55]

It has been repeatedly alleged that the development corporations have suppressed African business initiatives. The president of the National African Chamber of Commerce, Mr. S. Motsuenyane, has criticised the BIC for "interference and unfair competition."[56] Quite apart from their limited access to loans, African enterprises are restricted by the refusal of trading licences. The Minister of the Interior in each bantustan government wields enormous political power by the exercise of patronage: granting bottle-store licences, general dealer and dry cleaning licences and so on.[57] In BophuthaTswana, Chief Mangope used this weapon against all the traders in the bantustan at independence, almost all of them non-Tswanas who were refusing to accept BophuthaTswana citizenship (see Chapter 3).

There is yet another obstacle in the way of Africans developing their own enterprises inside the bantustans: the many cases where protests from white commercial interests have led to the government refusing permission for Africans to set up businesses and trading stores dealing in essential commodities, where the whites have hitherto enjoyed a monopoly of the African market in the bantustans. These pressures have prevented the construction of essential infrastructure, such as the extension of the railway south of Umtata in the Transkei. White bakers have blocked the issue of licences to African bakers in the bantustan township of Mdantsane, which serves East London. In the Eastern Transvaal in 1970, white farmers blocked the production and marketing of tomatoes on a government irrigation scheme in the bantustans.[58] In Natal white entrepreneurs are establishing their own factories and bottling plants outside the bantustan boundaries, and giving franchise rights for distribution to non-Africans. Chief Buthelezi has complained:

"Everyone but the African is talking about exploiting the African market ... What do we get out of all this? Can anyone deny that we are being reserved for the sole exploitation by people other than our own entrepreneurs?"[59]

It appears that the bantustans have been made into a protected reserve for Afrikaner capital, at least as far as management of the Bantu authority and bantustan accounts are concerned. A particularly blatant move was the awarding in 1973 of the R50 million a year account of the West Rand Bantu Administration Board to Volkskas; nearly all the 29 new Boards were also moving their accounts there. In the Transkei the bantustan government accounts, the XDC accounts and the Transkei Township Board accounts were all moved to Volkskas in spite of the superior services and terms offered by other commercial banks. According to banking circles, it appears that all the accounts of bodies dealing with African administration, whether in the bantustans or the urban township areas, were moving to Volkskas — a bank very closely identified with state corporations in South Africa and with government personalities — and that the decision to do this was being taken by the South African officials in the bantustan administrations who were refusing to put the accounts to open tender or to observe the wishes of the bantustan governments.[60]

It is in this context, perhaps, that one can understand the satisfaction expressed by Mr. M. C. Botha, former Minister of Bantu Affairs and Development, with regard to progress in the bantustans:

"We are honestly doing each day, today, tomorrow and next year, as much as they can absorb, as much as our means, manpower, time and intellects enable us to do."[61]

With the new emphasis on "development" on a grand scale in the bantustans, the sordid details of how the corporations run their affairs are being overshadowed by major new projects. One of the most popular is the construction of casinos and tourist facilities — for the rich, i.e. mainly those living well outside the bantustans themselves. The casino and luxury holiday complex at Mmabatho, in BophuthaTswana, has been described in Chapter 3; other similar ventures include a R700,000 (£400,000) hotel opened in 1978 in QwaQwa and hailed by the Chief Minister as the first step towards making his bantustan "an international playground".[62] A R10 million (£5.7m.) ski and holiday resort, complete with snow-making machines fed by three reservoirs, is also under way with backing from West German sources; work started in 1976.[63] Chief Minister Mopeli said in 1977 that the tourist development had been promised to QwaQwa on condition its government agreed to accept "internal autonomy."[64] Another casino and holiday complex is under construction on the Transkei coast under a franchise from Holiday Inns, 50% of it owned by the Transkei Development Corporation; the total cost is expected to be around R25 million.[65]

Another favourite kind of project for the development corporations is the construction of harbours, one for the Ciskei and one for the Transkei (the only two bantustans with any real access to the sea). These harbours duplicate existing facilities along the nearby coastline and have been heavily criticised as being an extravagant waste of money. In the case of the Transkei and its proposed "duty-free harbour" the only possible area, around Port St. Johns, is completely silted up and would need a phenomenal amount of dredging; in addition the "Wild Coast" on either side, as it is popularly known, is rugged and notoriously danger-ous to shipping. Dr. Panigel, a French entrepreneur who has sold the idea to the Transkei government, estimated the port would cost R125 million (£71m.) but a more realistic sum is estimated to be about £350 million.[66] It seems that the Transkei Development Corporation has turned down the scheme, which was then sold to the Transkei government.[67] In view of the Transkei's near-bankruptcy it seems unlikely that the project will get off the ground, but sub-stantial costs are likely to be involved in cancellation charges. Dr. Panigel has also established a lucrative connection with the Transkei government, which has contracted with him to co-ordinate the building of hospitals and clinics and the upgrading of present medical facilities for which he earns a percentage of the total costs — hardly an incentive to keep costs down to what the Transkei can afford.[68]

The Ciskei is also planning to build a new port, which Chief Minister Sebe boasts "will be bigger and better than East London harbour," on the site of Hamburg, now a remote holiday village for whites only on the Keiskamma River. Engineers and ecologists are sceptical about the merits of trying to develop this massively expensive duplicate of East London, which occupies the best natural site, since it would destroy a major fish-breeding ground and, because of the river estuary's narrow mouth and huge mud flats (similar to Port St. John's), the cost of keeping the harbour silt-free would be enormous.[69] Meanwhile, the white owners are being bought out at sometimes outrageously high prices by the development corporations. There has been much criticism of certain land deals at Port St. Johns and other parts of the Eastern Cape, where it was alleged the proper procedures had not been followed and that certain owners had been paid sums far in excess of the amounts they had themselves paid for the properties not long before.[70]

Other "development" projects are aimed at the interests only of whites. Particularly conspicuous in this regard is the expenditure of R4 million (£2.3m.) on a new road to bypass part of Lebowa, so that the local white farmers would not have to risk being disciplined by African police if they infringed traffic rules on their way through the bantustan. Their local Member of Parliament explained that his constituents "find it hard being stopped by a Bantu" and that "we're going to build a road that runs outside Lebowa to get around the problem."[71]

In some cases, it seems that "development" means the building of camps to accommodate people bulldozed out of squatter areas, whether by the South African government alone or with the help of the bantustan government as in BophuthaTswana. Here, an early estimate of the cost of rehousing only the Tswana refugees with permits for the area was around R36 million (£20.5m.), and the BophuthaTswana government has in fact earmarked land for the purpose; however, the problem has now trebled and it would cost at least R100 million (£57m.) to resettle people at the site, Soshanguve (formerly Mabopane East).[72]

Some of the ambitious projects already undertaken by the development corporations have been conspicuously unsuccessful. This was the case, for example, with the three major supermarket developments under way in Kwa-Zulu, under the control of the KwaZulu Development Corporation (KDC). A total of between R15 million (£8.6m.) and R17 million (£9.7m.) was involved in the case of these projects, which were suddenly suspended in August 1978 for re-examination of the plans. Leading professional sources blamed the delays on poor planning by KDC officials "out of their depth", and foresaw a considerable waste of money: "This is what happens when you get an 'in-house' type of thinking in the State corporations. This seems to be a case where public officials did not know how to carry schemes of this magnitude to full fruition." A completed supermarket in Madadeni, the first of its kind in KwaZulu, showed the estimates of local purchasing power to have been hopelessly optimistic, resulting in a turn-over way below that forecast.[73]

"Irregularities" have also been discovered at a factory owned by the BophuthaTswana National Development Corporation (BNDC) and the Corporation for Economic Development (CED), the former BIC under a new guise. During an investigation by auditors, which followed complaints from local competitors, it was found that the manager of the furniture factory had been using the facilities for his own private deals.[74] In other BIC/CED ventures there have been a rash of liquidations; in 1977 it was announced that the BIC had lent R18.8 million to companies which had since gone into liquidation. In six months, five manufacturers at the BIC's main development area at Babalegi, Bophutha-Tswana, had either gone into liquidation or been placed under judicial manage-ment.[75] The question was raised as to how thoroughly the BIC/CED investigated a company's viability before it agreed to build a factory tailored to that company's special requirements. In one case the company involved had a record of dis-astrous attempts at decentralisation.[76]

Developing the land

The South African government's attitude to agricultural development in the bantustans was shown in a very poor light when questions were raised recently about the use of surplus water from the enormous Orange River scheme for the

106

nearby Ciskei, which badly needed the water for its Tyefu agricultural scheme and the proposed resettlement camp at Glenmore. Water is also desperately needed at Thornhill, another resettlement camp where rural development of some sort is imperative. The South African Minister of Water Affairs, Mr. Braam Raubenheimer, told a questioner in the House of Assembly:

"We will have to look to our own needs before we can make our Orange River water available for the development of the Ciskei. The water will then be so expensive it will probably have to be used for industrial or other development."[77]

The only water scheme in the Ciskei will in fact provide only for white-owned industries brought in by the local development corporation at Dimbaza and Middledrift.[78]

There are a number of agricultural projects in the bantustans, but they are unlikely to resolve many of the bantustans' problems, if any at all. In the first place, like the other projects of the development corporations they are very badly planned and executed. A director of the Transkei Development Corporation, Prof. Graven, has admitted that quite large sums have been invested in dams and irrigation systems in the Transkei with little or no initial research having been done on the agronomic problems involved:

"The lack of reliable advance information on the suitability of the schemes for the production of specific crops has placed both the agricultural division of the TDC and the Ministry of Agriculture in the invidious position of having to base their decisions regarding the crops to be grown and the production practices to be applied on results of experiments conducted and experience gained under vastly different ecological conditions. Despite the appointment of renowned authorities as consultants, the lack of reliable local information has led to costly mistakes."[79]

The projects are also conceived on the basis of what is in South Africa's interest, not that of the people inside the bantustans. In its 1978 annual report, where the CED was itself admitting a crisis in bantustan agriculture and a possible major food shortage, it announced that it had vast projects which were focused mainly on the production of tea and coffee, in order to reduce the overall South African reliance on imports of these items. Projects to be launched in the bantustans over the next five years by the CED would aim to increase present coffee production, particularly of the high-grade arabica variety, by more than five times, and also provide about 80% of total tea consumption.[80]

The corporation was also now involved in a new "project farming" scheme which would enable white farmers to use land inside the bantustans, as agents of the corporations.[81] The agricultural projects involve tea-growing in Venda, game and cotton in Gazankulu, stock-fattening in KwaZulu, fish-farming and milk production in BophuthaTswana, and an irrigation project and milk production in the Ciskei. Substantial numbers of Africans are employed on these estates and have in effect been transformed from subsistence farmers to wage labourers on bantustan land.[82] A new major estate project is Zebediela Estates, a very large citrus-exporting venture bordering on Lebowa, which is to be bought by the Bantu Trust. The United Party objected that the R8 million purchase only served to transfer ownership of the land from a private corporation to a government corporation, and should not count as land to be added to the bantustans under the 1936 Land Act; it did not even provide any additional jobs for Africans.[83]

The beneficiaries of these "development" projects are the development corporations themselves, the white farmers involved and perhaps some of the bantustan Ministers. Allegations have been made that two farms belonging to the Bantu Trust were being occupied and farmed free of rent in the Transkei by Chief Minister (now President) Matanzima and his brother George. At Chief Matanzima's request the Transkei Development Corporation was about to hand over a third farm for the use of the Minister of Finance, Mr. Letlaka. All three farms were being run by the TDC and it seems that Matanzima intended taking possession as soon as they were transferred from South Africa to Transkei. The Deputy Minister for Bantu Development said his Department had authorised Matanzima to occupy a house on the farm, but refused to comment on the other allegations. George Matanzima did not deny any of the allegations, but tended to confirm them : "Of course the Prime Minister, who worked so hard to acquire the land, will be among the beneficiaries, and so will his brother."[84]

By far the most important beneficiaries of this new style of agricultural development are the white farmers. This has been a highly contentious issue in the Ciskei, starting with the whites' outcry at the proposal for consolidating the Ciskei into four areas; they argued that it conflicted with the policy of the Cape Province of expanding the exclusive rights of whites in the areas concerned.[85] These pressures led to all consolidation plans being based on agreements with local white farmers' associations — in Natal, for example, with the Natal Agricultural Union[86] — in complete disregard of the principle that consolidation be in line with the interests of bantustan development. Even after incorporation of new areas into the bantustans, the whites manage to retain control under the new system. The Ciskei's Chief Minister, Lennox Sebe, complained that the Ciskei bantustan existed only on paper, a "fantasia created out of words, phrases and political gimmicks," since vast areas remained firmly in the hands of white farmers. Areas bought by the South African Bantu Trust were leased back to their former owners, or to other white entrepreneurs "at nominal rentals."[87] Sebe repeated the attack a year later, after the South African government had refused to take any notice of his protests, and accused them of:

"Buying land from whites and re-leasing it back to the same or different whites supposedly in the name of homeland development, hanging on, refusing to let go the reins of control, adopting a dog in the manger attitude with trust land and openly claiming these lands must be given over to the development corporation and other entrepreneurs for safe keeping . . .[88]

It seems that white farmers are there in the bantustans to stay. Dr. Ferdie Hartzenburg, Deputy Minister of Plural Relations, actually claimed in 1978 that

KwaZulu's strongest asset was the innumerable white farming areas running through it.[89]

The ordinary people shut up in the bantustans with little or no land would probably not agree, although their voice is not recorded in the way that Hartzenburg's and the white farmers' are. Increasingly, the people are being reduced to the level of landless labourers who can survive only by selling themselves to the nearest white farmer, one day at a time. This is a problem particularly affecting women — who, as mentioned in Chapter 5, are usually not allocated any land — and children, many of whom have been completely separated from their fathers or sometimes from both parents by the migrant labour system. In KaNgwane it was reported that many people were being transported daily to work in the fields of white farms, most of them being women and young children.[90] Mr. Botha had earlier stated his determination not to allow people to settle on the land in KaNgwane until it had been completely planned for "development as an entity."[91] The same effect was reported by the *Financial Mail* in KwaZulu:

"Parents send their children to work on neighbouring white farms, and the FM watched a truck driver deliver its overflowing cargo of children aged nine and ten to their homes at the end of the day's work. One child told the FM that his friends were paid with potatoes that could fill the equivalent of three Coke tins."[92]

This same journal, however, had also managed to comment warmly on the "courageous KwaZulu government policy decisions to make better use of land" by removing the people from it.[93]

The problems of African farmers in the bantustans continue to mount under the pressures to "develop" their land, in the interests of others. Additional burdens are imposed by the imposition of livestock taxes by bantustan governments anxious to squeeze more money out of the people for their "development" projects, under threat of confiscating their animals if they fail to produce the cash. In Transkei, a farmer told a reporter that his animals were crucial in working his small plot of land to feed his family, providing milk, power for the plough, transport and various local transactions. There was no money to pay the tax, or the general tax which had been raised from R1 a year to R10: "Some Ministers are buying up farms and homes and those of us who battle very hard to earn a living are being fleeced."[94] A farmer caught in the same dilemma in KwaZulu saw it as the end of the agricultural way of life:

"And now they are killing us. They are putting a tax on our livestock. To pay the tax we will have to go to town to work. Sofa! Nya! Nya! We shall die. With tax like that no-one will want to farm. No Black person will ever be a farmer. We weep for ourselves."[95]

For white farmers there is an unlimited supply of credit from the Land Bank, subsidies for good conservation practices, and co-operatives for cheap fertiliser, seed and wire as well as outlets for any surplus produce: all components of a useful agricultural development strategy. For African farmers in the bantustans there is nothing except mounting taxes on their pitifully small resources, even where they have some land and livestock. Increasingly, they are losing both. It is hardly surprising that the "development" of the bantustans is driving farmers away from farming and making it something to be avoided at all costs, as the CED is complaining.[96]

Decentralisation of industry

With the decline in subsistence agriculture as the basis for the local economy, together with the relentless increases in population as a result of removals from the urban area, white farms and other bantustans, the need to provide some kind of substitute economy in the bantustans is vital. Increasing importance has been given to the decentralisation of white industry from the industrial centres of South Africa to the "border areas" adjoining the bantustans, and later certain "growth points" inside. By the end of 1971, in fact, the government was claiming that sole responsibility for making the bantustans economically viable rested with private industry:

"One of the attitudes that will have to change is that the government should be solely responsible for the development of the homelands . . . Without the contribution of the necessary know-how and enterprise all our offers of money will be of no or little avail."[97]

The major industrial areas of South Africa — the Western Cape, Port Elizabeth-Uitenhage, Durban-Pinetown and the Southern Transvaal — concentrate 81% of all secondary industry into 3% of the country's area. The border industries programme was announced by Dr. Verwoerd in 1965:

"White factories on the perimeter of reserved African areas would make full use of tribal African workers, who would thus be absorbed there in the service of white people".[98]

It was optimistically forecast that by this means the nine or ten million additional African population then projected by the end of the century (subsequently rejected as a gross underestimate) would be settled outside the concentration of whites, to ensure the latters' "safety."[99] Even then, however, there was no serious plan for the removal of already employed Africans from the "white areas." It has since been realized also that the official assumptions of each employed African providing direct support for four others, with a further "multiplier" effect to support 25 people indirectly, was a wild overestimate.[100] In practice, most of the jobs in border industries have simply been moved short distances to the cheapest and most accessible areas very near the industrial complexes, and involve no new employment creation anywhere near the main bantustan areas. One of the main border areas is at Rosslyn, near Pretoria, and there are others near Durban, Pietermaritzburg and East London. Because of this, no "multiplier" effect on production of goods and services for local consumption in the bantustans has been observed. Professor Lombard, a noted Afrikaner theorist and apologist for apartheid, has pointed out:

"Unfortunately these large Bantu towns, the major potential growth poles of their respective hinterlands, have thus far remained satellites of their economically further advanced white poles. Instead of giving rise to multiplier effects on further domestic employment in the homelands, as Dr. Verwoerd expected they would do, incomes from labour are, for the most part, 'leaking back' to the Republican poles of activity."[101]

It seems to be generally accepted that the border areas, far from providing an economic boost to the bantustans, are probably harmful because wages are spent in the nearby "white area", and they drain away any skills, labour and investment that might otherwise be available inside the bantustan.[102] Dr. A. S. Jacobs, a well-known Afrikaner economist and former adviser to the Prime Minister, has commented:

"It is often said that the border areas have a negative influence on the development of the Bantu area. I have a lot of sympathy with this point of view, because the border areas are situated close to the Bantu areas and yet the Bantu are not allowed to do skilled work."[103]

Partly because of opposition to forced decentralisation by industry, the border area programme has been de-emphasised in the 1970s. In fact the South African government's own stake in decentralised areas is less than 10% of total investment there, in spite of its overwhelming potential for directing state corporations and related operations to the border areas.[104] There have been complaints from investors of "extreme and unnecessary difficulties" resulting from a lack of co-ordination of planning in the border areas, including "regular power and water failures," inadequate telecommunications and transportation, and a lack of housing for workers.[105] The "model" decentralised township of Berlin, on the border of Ciskei near East London, is "almost wholly unsuccessful", according to the *Financial Mail*, and the loan from the East London Council may not be recoverable.[106] Following a marked slowdown in the rate of decentralisation in 1972,[107] enforcement of the Physical Planning Act, which requires that all industries employing a large proportion of Africans move to border areas, has been quietly relaxed. The *Financial Gazette* has pointed out that the trend is towards increasing centralisation as part of the rationalisation of production and marketing.[108]

The border areas remain the most important focus of decentralisation, but there is now a programme for the establishment of industry within the bantustans. The *Financial Mail* reacted to the new policy of allowing investment there by saying that the various tax and other incentives were greatly outweighed by the disadvantages, of which the most serious were the total lack of infrastructure in the bantustans, except for fragments very close to the cities, and the uncertainties involved with regard to raw materials, labour, training facilities and other basics.[109] Moreover, Mr. M. C. Botha has announced that the subsidies and price preferences on bantustan industries' contracts with his department would be available only for a few "growth points", or sites which would not involve the BIC in "excessive" expenditure on basic services.[110]

The first of the "growth centres" is Babalegi, nominally within one of the pieces of the BophuthaTswana bantustan but only 20 miles north of Pretoria. It is a bantustan showcase; in 1973, for example, the former French Prime Minister, M. Antoine Pinay, was reported to be so impressed by the industrial development there that he said he would recommend French investment in the bantustans on his return. The *Financial Mail*, however criticised Pinay's judgement about Babalegi:

"The reality is far less impressive. The first industrialists moved into Babalegi three years ago. Today, although all available space is occupied or booked, only half of it has been developed.

"The Bantu Investment Corporation's annual report for 1969-70 forecast that, by the end of 1971, some 70 companies would be employing at least 8,000 Blacks. So far, there are 52 concerns (36 of them small ones operated in factory flats) employing 5,000 Blacks. With a work-force in the area of 40,000 or more, the Black employment target for Babalegi is 10,000.

"The picture at Isitebe (the second growth point, also fully booked) is even less encouraging . . . Employment target for the first phase of development is 4,000 — 5,000. So far seven factories have opened, employing 1,000 Blacks. They are expected to provide another 400 jobs."[111]

By the end of 1978 it had become apparent that even such progress as had been made with decentralisation at the time of Pinay's visit was a short-lived phenomenon. From 1977 onwards, the CED's Dr. Adendorff has admitted that the creation or transfer of jobs for Africans in decentralised areas is completely inadequate for meeting the increase in unemployment inside the bantustans, let alone to support the development of border industry.[112]

In the attempt to bypass the lack of interest shown by companies in South Africa, the development corporations have advertised extensively abroad, particularly in the United States, Britain, France and West Germany. The promotions concentrate heavily on the use of bantustan Chief Ministers as symbols of bantustan progress. Local entrepreneurs have complained that this advertising campaign abroad, where there is little direct knowledge of what the bantustans are like, is a way of putting pressure on them to decentralise.[113] A popular place to invest is KwaZulu,[114] where overseas investors in particular can claim the support of Chief Minister Buthelezi, the bantustan personality who has received the most positive publicity internationally. The giant liquor group Seagrams, for example, ignored opposition at home in the United States to investing in Kwa-Zulu by quoting the endorsement of Buthelezi.[115] Among the multi-national companies involved in the bantustans are Laborbau, Bayer, Machinen-fabrik and the Spilo group of West Germany; ITT, General Electric and King Resources of the United States; GEC, Lonrho, Barclays and Standard Bank of Britain; Peugeot of France; Peter Hartmann of Switzerland; the East Asiatic Co. of Denmark; and the Quebec Iron and Titanium Corporation, a Canadian subsidiary of the American Kennecott Copper Corporation. Nearly 40% of all private capital invested in the bantustans now comes from overseas sources,[116] a major benefit to South Africa's balance of payments as well as its bantustan policy.

The bantustans' "growth points" cannot solve the problem of economic unviability for the bantustans as a whole, but merely create a new urban squatter problem in the vicinity of the major urban centres at places which are only nominally inside a bantustan. Economically they operate in the same way as the border areas, with earnings being spent in the nearby "white areas," while they drain off all available capital for "development" supposedly authorised for the bantustans in general rather than areas which are bantustans in name only. Their major impact is to depress the level of African wages, since minimum wage determinations are waived for Africans in bantustan areas. Strikes are in effect illegal in the bantustans although there have nevertheless been some strikes in protest at low wages. In BophuthaTswana, for example, more than 100 workers at Babalegi Industries struck over their minimal wages of R5 (£2.85) a week, with no increments for experience or extra skills. One of the strikers, Violet Tshabalala, said it was impossible to live on the wages:

"I left this factory because it was hell trying to live on R5 a week with the cost of living so high [prices are comparable with Europe]. I might as well stay at home."[117]

The strike was illegal, and the manager, Mr. Falkson, threatened to smash a reporter's camera if they "dared" to photograph him.[118]

Wages even lower than in the rest of South Africa are deliberately being promoted to investors as a major reason for investing in the bantustans. An official survey published by the government and designed to attract investment to the bantustans and border industries showed that wage rates in the main growth points were far below the Poverty Datum Line and below the rates paid in "white areas." Wage Board minimum levels are set for the "white areas" but do not apply to either border areas or bantustans. Compared to the minimum unskilled wage of R13 a week, average rates in the growth points were mostly between R6.50 and R10.[119] African wages in the border area of Rustenburg are up to 64% below those paid in the main urban centres.[120]

One of the biggest employers in the bantustans, Kool Look Wigs at Babalegi, employs about 600 workers, mainly women, at a basic wage of R4 a week and average of R6 a week; there is no pension fund, medical assistance, transport or paid sick leave. The Poverty Datum Line at Babalegi, R18 a week, is three times the average wage at Kool Look.[121]

A survey of the wage situation in the decentralised growth points concludes that the policy "is having a negative effect on the standard of living of the Blacks."[122]

The South African Minister of Economic Affairs, Mr. C. Heunis, instructed the Legislative Assembly in Lebowa not to put off prospective investors coming to Lebowa by demanding that they respect the interests of the people there. "Tactless, unrealistic and sensational demands and ill-timed emotional utterances by the leaders of a country can do a great deal of harm."[123] A CED advertisement for investment in Gazankulu advertised its "many glittering attributes" which included "an eager and industrious labour force."[124]

Among the most industrious are the women in the bantustans, who are becoming the major wage-labour force there since they can be hired for even lower rates than the men.[125] The Transkei has institutionalised this with minimum wages for men more than 50% higher than for women.[126] The women have virtually no prospect of access to the towns except as domestic servants, where they are isolated, very poorly paid and separated from their children. Being virtually imprisoned in the bantustan, and directly responsible for the survival of children and other dependants in the absence of most able-bodied men, their desperate need for some kind of income can be readily exploited. Women earn substantially less than men while doing many of the hard jobs that men are doing in the white areas: construction work, road-building and factory work. One construction foreman in KwaZulu boasted that "his women" were "good workers", "never loaf" and "always turn up to work". If one of them had to stay away, a friend or relative invariably stood in for her.[127] Given the desperate need for jobs, it is obvious that the workers are subject to enormous pressures from their governments to support the ruling party regardless of their own inclinations. This affected several thousand people working in the Babalegi growth-point in BophuthaTswana, who were told at the time of the bantustan's independence not to return to work unless they applied for citizenship, thereby of course forfeiting their South African citizenship to which, as non-Tswanas, they were still entitled and which they were very unwilling to give up. The threat to fire people who did not take out citizenship of the bantustan was confirmed by a representative of one of the factories in the area and by the local chief.[128]

The South African government's original justification for its attempt to force Africans back into the bantustans or border areas to work, as well as to live, was that they could develop their own talents in their own areas, free of the restrictions of job reservation in the "white areas". However, this promise has been completely reversed under pressure from the white trade unions. As demanded by Mr. L. J. van den Berg, the President of the Afrikaners' trade union federation, the Koordinerende Raad van S.A. Vakverenigings:

"Everyone must be made to realize that a border area remains a white area and that the development of border areas aims only at the decentralisation of industries."[129]

Aside from the exclusion of Africans from skilled jobs, there is also the other side of job reservation in the bantustans and border areas, namely the maintenance of a strict ration of white to black workers to guarantee jobs for whites whether they are needed or not. Starting in 1970, new job reservation specifications to this effect were introduced at Rosslyn, the largest border area, for the motor assembly industry on the recommendations of the Industrial Council for the industry after representations by the white workers.[130] Although statutory job reservation was all but abolished in 1979, the "white preference" policy is maintained in many industrial agreements.

The disruption of migrant labour, which the provision of jobs in and near the bantustans was originally supposed to eliminate, continues to be an important factor because of the distances between the border areas and bantustan "growth points," which are on the fringes of the main existing industrial areas, and the concentrations of bantustan population. Only 20% of the labour force in one of the BophuthaTswana platinum mines, for example, are local Tswanas,[131] and as many as 75% are from outside South Africa itself.[132]

Mining the bantustans

As originally conceived, the African reserves were conspicuous for their total lack of mineral resources. Where minerals were found, as with the copper at Phalaborwa, an ancient African mining centre, the area was simply removed from the reserve.[133] A strip of coast excised from the KwaZulu bantustan for "development" purposes in March 1975 has R2,000 million worth of titanium in its sand-dunes; it could yield more metal than the total current world output, and is now being exploited by US and Canadian corporations in partnership with the South African government's Industrial Development Corporation.[134] The asbestos mine at Penge is in a "white area" in the middle of Lebowa. Some African landowners in various areas are being evicted so that whites can have access to suspected mineral deposits.[135]

In several bantustans, however, minerals have been discovered since the establishment of the boundaries. Where this happens the boundaries may be kept as they are, and mining operations started for all practical purposes are the same as those in any other part of the Republic. All their agreements have been with the South African government and its agencies, including the Bantu Mining Corporation. While technically the companies operate in the bantustans on a temporary basis, former Prime Minister Vorster made it clear they they will be encouraged to remain until the deposits are exhausted:

"In the case of a mining industry which undertakes development there on an agency basis, one would have to make the agency arrangement for the longer term, depending upon the mineral and the life of the mine. In that case, for example, 50 years would not be an unreasonable figure".[136]

Mining leases have been granted for a number of deposits in the bantustans, particularly BophuthaTswana and Lebowa. It is very unclear whether any significant revenue accrues to any of the bantustan governments in the form of licences, taxes or royalties; in many cases payments are made to the South African government and its agencies such as the Bantu Mining Corporation or Bantu Trust. When asked what revenue was accruing to governments or individuals inside the bantustans, the Minister of Bantu Administration stated, surprisingly, that "the required particulars are unfortunately not available" and added that the matters were the concern of the bantustan governments themselves — a dubious proposition since such information as the total value of production was available, and in view of the dominant role taken by its own agencies.[137]

As with the decentralisation of industry, the early promises that Africans could develop their own resources without the restraints of job reservation have proved

115

worthless for mine-workers in the bantustans. The powerful, whites-only Mine Workers' Union operates a closed shop in South African and Namibian mines and it has refused to train or allow Africans to join the union, the key to access to the skilled and highly-paid jobs; the Government has upheld this colour bar.[138] The situation is summed up by the *Financial Mail*:

"There is no difference between a mine in the homelands and a mine in the white area as far as job restrictions . . . are concerned. The skilled workers are the Whites pulling in the high wages; Blacks are alongside them underground, the drillers and shovel men. They remain unskilled not because they are incapable of doing more responsible jobs, but because they are not allowed to . . ."[139]

This issue has produced something of a crisis in BophuthaTswana since its independence, raising the issue of whether the bantustan controls the mines or perhaps the other way around. Relations with the two major platinum mining operations, Rustenburg and Impala Platinum, were extremely cordial at independence, the South African Chamber of Mines having provided the independence stadium (a temporary structure easily dismantled) for the whole ceremony.[140] The following year, however, questions began to be raised about the Mine Workers' Union refusal to allow Africans to qualify in any mining skills, ignoring various Ministers' claims that this would be a top priority for the newly independent bantustan, and at the same time there were a couple of incidents where white miners clashed with bantustan police, the major case being one where a white man from the Impala mine claimed to have been pushed around by an African policeman in a charge office, during questioning about an assault on a black worker.[141] These incidents were immediately taken up by the Mine Workers' Union and its boss, the hard-line Mr. Arrie Paulus, with a threat of strike action or even pulling out all union members from the bantustan and so leaving the mines crippled.[142] Mr. Paulus pointed out that the mines could not bring in miners from overseas because of the closed-shop agreement, and demanded that the BophuthaTswana government take action to protect his members: "It is up to them to repeal the laws."[143] At the same time, he repeated his members' determination not to train Africans. The South African Mines and Works Act was still in effect in BophuthaTswana, making it impossible for an African to qualify for a blasting certificate, the key to promotion from the lowest labouring levels in the mine. BophuthaTswana has refrained from repealing the Act so far in order not to antagonise the MWU; there is some talk of doing so, but it would require two years' notice and in any case have little effect in the light of the all-powerful union's refusal to train Africans or allow the employment of any non-members in jobs they regard as theirs.[144]

The numbers game: employment in the border areas and bantustans

Since the incentives for decentralisation are generally proportional to the capital expenditure involved, there is a tendency for investment in border areas and bantustans to be extremely capital-intensive; the cost of providing a job is high, and increasing. This is not only a well-known phenomenon in various decentralisation schemes in Britain and elsewhere, but is also related to South Africa's lack of experience in economic planning of this kind; the result is the opposite of that intended, namely to provide jobs in or near the bantustans. As Professor Lombard has observed:

"The South African public and its administration have no tradition of continuous planning for collective economic goals far removed from trends and patterns caused by the automatic operation of the market mechanism.[145]

Total expenditure by the BIC since the programme of industrial development in the bantustans was launched up to 1974 was R41 million, and resulted in the creation of only 9,000 new jobs,[146] a cost per job for the BIC alone of R4,556. The investment by industrialists also tends to produce few jobs; a major new venture, a chemical plant in the Transkei which started production in 1974, cost R1.6 million to create only 200 black jobs, at an average cost of R8,000 each.[147] The average cost of creating a job in the bantustans between 1962 and 1968 was R11,500.[148] This is far higher than the cost of jobs in the "white areas." The figures, moreover, are based on development of the most convenient and cheapest locations, near existing industrial areas and far removed from the major concentrations of the bantustan population.

At this level of investment required for each new job, the financial provisions for employment creation in the bantustans and border areas cannot make any impact on the mounting unemployment which is becoming perhaps the dominant feature of the bantustans. Between 1962 and 1972 about 8,500 new jobs were created in the bantustans and border areas each year while between 60,000 and 70,000 new male work-seekers a year were coming into the labour market from the bantustans alone.[149] The Tomlinson Commission estimated that the reserves could support 7 million people at subsistence level provided there was comprehensive agricultural development together with 1,250,000 new jobs there. By 1970 the 7 million had already been crowded onto the bantustans, but less than 5% of the jobs called for in the border areas and bantustans had been provided.[150]

Thus the policy of decentralising industry in the border areas and bantustans works to undermine African employment generally, in a double action. Firstly, investment is diverted into moving jobs or creating a relatively small number compared to what could have been achieved in the areas where industry is already established. It has been estimated that by 1980 nearly 4 million Africans, out of a working population of 10 million, will be unemployed.[151] Secondly, by allowing decentralised industry to undercut even the low wages paid in the "white areas," the general level of African wages in South Africa is depressed further. Inadequate wages and outright unemployment, therefore, are problems which are exacerbated by the bantustan policy.

Unemployment reserves for migrant labour

In a 1974 study of the attitudes of people confined to the bantustans, deep distrust was recorded of the South African government's intentions in implementing the bantustan policy. There was resentment at the omnipresent white control of bantustan affairs, as well as forced tribal separation and removals. The bitterest criticism, however, hinges on the lack of economic and social advances, and the feeling that the acute shortage of jobs, houses and schools is actually becoming worse. Unanimous blame for this "backwardness" has been placed on white South Africa for exploiting Africans as cheap labour by reducing the bantustans to acute poverty.[152]

A survey of migrant workers from the Transkei and Ciskei in Cape Town by the economists Janet Graaff and Johann Maree showed that the workers and their families had very little or no land for cultivation and few or no livestock; almost all of them could barely survive, if at all, on what they could earn inside the bantustan. A quarter of all the families had no income and no resources of any kind.[153] This absolute poverty explains the desperation with which women will take the most poorly-paid jobs in the whole of South Africa, and men will seek work in the "white areas" where pay is a little better, either through defying the pass laws to go to the towns or haunting the bantustan labour bureaux in search of a job. It is reported from Umtata, Transkei, that whenever recruiting truck drivers arrive in the Transkei towns, hundreds of desperate men who have been seeking employment for months, clamour round in frantic attempts to get jobs.[154] At Dimbaza, Ciskei, which is the main "growth point" there, an advertised job at the local foundry drew 1,500 applications — almost a quarter of the entire adult population of the town. Every day both women and men line the fences of the few factory sites in the hope of getting a little work.[155] The labour bureaux can, and do, exploit the need for jobs by allowing people to register as workseekers only for one category of work — unpopular kinds such as working on white farms, where wages and conditions are particularly grim, or the mines.[156] Regardless of whatever kind of work a person may have done previously, once registered as a farm labourer he or she is condemned for life to work for white farmers in order to leave the bantustan.

Describing the historical evolution of migrant labour, the sociologist Pierre van den Berghe writes:

". . . Africans have not only lost most of their land to the Whites; they have also been forced out of their remaining Reserves, not fundamentally because of the 'lure of the city,' or opportunities for higher wages, but rather because migration was an imperative necessity for sheer physical survival."

He gives special emphasis to the fact that South African government policy has kept African workers in a constant, two-way migration between the reserves and the economic centres, preventing a gradual adjustment of traditional society to the modern sector:

"Through the large-scale use of migrant labour by much of White industry, the social change brought about by economic forces has been much more traumatic and disruptive of traditional peasant society than would have been the case with gradual, one-way migration. First, the African migrant worker is separated from his family for long periods; and, second, cyclical two-way

migration necessarily involves a much greater proportion of the population in a shorter time space."[157]
Migrant labour, then dominates the life of the bantustans both from an economic and from a social point of view. At any one time, almost 35% of employable males theoretically resident in the bantustans are absent, while many others are waiting for jobs in the white areas.[158] Over 70% of the "economically active" population is involved in the migrant labour system.[159] A recent study indicates that it is the strongest and most able of the men who manage to leave the bantustans. In Venda, for example, the population between the ages of 30 and 39 is 84% women and between 40 and 49, 75% are women.[160]

Having no economic option except migrant labour, basic survival for Africans depends on access to the "white areas." Given freedom of movement, there is little doubt that millions of people would leave the bantustans. The increasing impoverishment of these areas, therefore, is probably the major reason for the retention of the complex network of pass laws and other restrictive legislation.

An article in the *Rand Daily Mail* described the bantustan system as becoming "a chain of labour reservoirs where people are held in a state of compulsory unemployment until the white economy wants them."[161]

The importance of the bantustans to the whole scheme for using African labour while attempting to segregate Africans in remote areas has always been stressed by the South African government in its policy formulations. At the beginning of the development of current bantustan ideology, Dr. Verwoerd described the concept to the House of Assembly:

"The Bantu homelands . . . may be areas which to a large extent (although the people live within their own areas and are governed there) are dependent on basic incomes earned in the adjoining white territory."[162]

CHAPTER 9

The Hard Sell

As has already been mentioned in this short study of the bantustans, one of the major preoccupations of the South African government and of the bantustan Ministers has been presenting a favourable image of the policy to the international community, despite the fact that this draws considerable funds, time and attention of those responsible away from the overwhelming problems facing the people already inside, and those being moved into or between the bantustans. It would be fair to say that the public relations exercise aimed at selling the bantustans is a direct contribution to the increasing poverty, sickness and despair for the people confined there.

The propaganda is getting through to the outside world; the realities of life in the bantustans are not. For example, a large expensive book *The Republic of Transkei*, full of glossy, full-colour photographs, has been sent to libraries in Britain free of charge and is displayed in some of them without any attempt to ensure that it is labelled as propaganda or to make other material on South Africa available to the reading public.[1]

Other widely disseminated and expensive books include Benbo's *Bophutha-Tswana at Independence; Homelands: The role of the Corporations in the Republic of South Africa;* and the Africa Institute's *Black Homelands in South Africa*. These are aimed primarily at non-South Africans, since they are so euphoric about the bantustans that local people reading the day-to-day news would probably find them unrecognisable.

Other publications from the South African Department of Information have also become a major channel for claims about the bantustans, under their various new titles. Additional credibility is provided by favourable press reporting, relying heavily on South African government versions of issues, and by the support of private companies, the most important of these being Barclays Bank which has produced a special issue of its "Business Guides" entitled *The Emerging States in South Africa*, presenting a very favourable view of "development" in the bantustans.

To an informed and critical reader, these publications have all the hallmarks of propaganda. *The Voice of Transkei No. 2* claims in relation to the supposed breaking-off of diplomatic relations with South Africa that "the youth of the Transkei . . . felt reassured that Dr. Matanzima was a real fighter and well worthy of their support. Thenceforth their support for him grew by leaps and bounds." Ostensibly more objective, Barclays Bank states categorically, "Riots and politically motivated unrest have been minimal in the emerging states . . . and generally the labour force is content."[2] Unsubstantiated claims are made with no evidence at all being produced, destined to be repeated many time by those who read the publications and claim therefore to know about the "emerging states." *The Republic of BophuthaTswana*, produced for the South African Department of Information, claims that the mining potential of the bantustan is "among the highest in Africa", the quality of the cattle is "far above the average for black Africa" and gross national income per capita is "higher than that of at least 30 independent states." The *Financial Mail* is frankly sceptical: "These interesting claims would carry more weight if the book cited evidence for them. It does not."[3]

It is not the intention here to examine in detail the arguments or the image advanced in the propaganda about the bantustans; merely to note that arguments for international recognition of their "independence" follow the familiar South African line that its policies should be accepted on the grounds that there are worse things happening elsewhere — the familiar and disreputable *tu quoque* argument. Faced with the necessity for rationalising the strangely arbitrary and constantly shifting geography of the bantustan fragments, South Africa often argues that there are some countries in the world which are smaller than some bantustans (although they might have difficulty finding one smaller than QwaQwa) and that the fact of their fragmentation into so many widely separated pieces is no worse than the position of a state which incorporates many scattered islands such as Denmark, the Philippines or Indonesia.[4] South Africans refrain from mentioning the unhappy instances of states composed of two parts separated by another state's territory, such as the former Pakistan or pre-war Poland and Italy. Also avoided is the delicate issue of the reassignment on an arbitrary basis of different fragments of land between bantustans; the uncertainty over the borders and their continually shifting nature as land 'swaps' proceed with the white areas; and, above all, the *combination* of small size, fragmentation, dependency on 'white' towns for most basic services, lack of economic viability, lack of real control by the nominal government, lack of coherent history as a territorial unit, forced transportation of South African citizens into the territory and even firm opposition to independence by the inhabitants, which make the bantustans uniquely deficient in the criteria for international recognition.

Creeping recognition?

With these fairly obvious points in mind, it is important to be aware that there are individuals and governments which are showing themselves very eager to believe the claims made about the bantustans; they will believe what they find in their interest, and the bantustans are an obvious place to start in providing respectability to South Africa's policy of separate development. A number of concessions have been made which comprise elements of recognition even while formal diplomatic recognition remains, for the time being, out of the question.

One of these elements concerns postage stamps; stamps from Transkei have been accepted by some Western countries as valid despite the absence of any formal agreement to this effect. Even more important is the acceptance of passports from the Transkei and BophuthaTswana bantustans, particularly in the case of their Chief Ministers and members of their Cabinets. Chief Matanzima has been able to claim that the Transkei is effectively recognised around the world by the acceptance of its passports: "We have travelled freely in Britain, the United States, France and Switzerland."[5] This has involved a major change of attitude, since at the time of Transkei's independence all the Western countries had said emphatically that Transkeian passports, as symbols of the denial of people's right to South African citizenship, would not be recognised.[6] In 1978 it was reported that a traveller to Greece using a Transkeian passport had been told that the Transkei had recently been added to the immigration officials' list of countries recognised by the Greek government.[7]

Such moves undermine the stand taken against the bantustans by the Organisation of African Unity and particularly by the two members most affected, Lesotho and Botswana. The Minister of Foreign Affairs of Lesotho, faced with pressure from South Africa to recognise the Transkei, announced:

"We totally reject the bantustans as nothing but the implementation of apartheid. They mean that the white man cannot live with the black man. We won't stamp the passports of these people because that would imply recognition."[8]

Soon after Transkei's independence, Lesotho complained that the border post used by many of its people for buying essential supplies had been closed to force it to recognise the Transkei. Many Lesotho citizens were also turned away in early 1978 on the grounds that they did not have Transkei entry documents — available only in Umtata and therefore impossible to obtain.[9] The United Nations has been providing special assistance to Lesotho, which is entirely surrounded by South Africa, to mitigate the effects of South Africa's withdrawal of its subsidies on grain for Lesotho, which would clearly hit the people living near the breadline in this very poor country.[10]

Botswana also has its problems, particularly with the independence of BophuthaTswana. The Botswana government has stated that it would not recognise the bantustan, but would give its citizens special permits to visit Botswana. The Ambassador to the United Nations referred to Lesotho's plea for international assistance following Transkeian independence, and stated that his country was likely to experience similar problems.[11]

South Africa has also attempted to induce other nations to recognise the Transkei through reciprocal visits. Ecuador, for example, sent an official delegation to the Transkei, with an invitation given to Matanzima to visit Ecuador in return.[12] There are contacts on an official level with Taiwan and Israel. Official visits have also been exchanged with the Ivory Coast, and it was reported that the possibility of eventual diplomatic relations was discussed.[13] Another of the French government's close allies in Africa, Senegal, has had contacts between its President Senghor and representatives of the BophuthaTswana government.[14] France itself is a major target of bantustan promotion; French firms, notably Les Grands Travaux de Marseille, are anxious to get involved in the Transkeian port venture and a major Transkeian delegation has been in France to visit key figures in industry and commerce. A French subsidiary of the Corporation for Economic Development (formerly the BIC) is to be opened up in Paris, under the name l'Association pour le Developpement de l'Industrie en Afrique.[15]

While failing to offer formal recognition, Britain and the United States have allowed various bantustan Chief Ministers to visit their countries, usually at the invitation of private interests, with all expenses paid and important introductions assured. The number of visits is too great to be detailed: for example Chief Mangope visited Britain in October 1977, shortly before BophuthaTswana became "independent", on a trip to talk to bankers and industrialists in Europe. His London press conference was organised by the South African Embassy.[16] In the United States Dr. Kissinger and President Carter had meetings with Chief Sebe of the Ciskei and Chief Buthelezi of KwaZulu respectively, while the latter is also in contact with Congressmen and members of the Administration.[17] There have been reports that white advisers appointed by three bantustan Chief Ministers, those of Ciskei, Lebowa and KwaZulu, have close links with American institutions.[18] Certainly the Quail Commission appointed to inquire into the desirability of Ciskeian independence had three American members and one Briton, Sir Arthur Snelling, former British ambassador to South Africa.[19]

The first known visit of a Western government representative to a bantustan was that of an Austrian official to the Transkei in July 1978; this was seen as a prelude to a major investment in the Transkei by one of Austria's largest industrial conglomerates, Steyr-Daimler-Puch. The company was planning to invest in the manufacture of bicycles and farming equipment, as well as some other projects that they "cannot talk about." Sources close to the firm were quoted as admitting that it manufactured firearms.[20] Backing up this official contact, the official Austrian Broadcasting and Television Corporation broadcast a 15-minute programme on Transkei; in Umtata, a Transkei Government Minister described this as the first case of "objective broadcasts about the Transkei"; the political commentator, Prof. Schlapp, had been extremely complimentary about the Transkei's independence and the merits of its Prime Minister, Kaiser Matanzima.[21] Another step to acceptability was provided by an invitation to a Transkei delegate to a "dialogue congress" of European and African countries held in Alpbach, Austria, in the month before the visit to Transkei. As a result of the prominence given to the Transkei speaker, an African specialist from Britain's Foreign and Commonwealth Office suggested an official contact between the Transkei and the British Ambassador in Pretoria.[22]

"Development" — a key to recognition?

A range of foreign companies is being invited to invest in the bantustans; some have been mentioned in Chapter 8. Projects are reported to involve West German, Israeli and unnamed Arab investors. The latter are said to be connected with Medi Dupis, a Middle Eastern financial consortium, through its representative Mr. Salim el Hajj, who is based in Beirut. A group of unidentified Arab interests were alleged to be involved in the deal, worth R440 million (£251m.) for the proposed Transkei harbour, airport, housing, tourist facilities and other "development" projects.[23] The CED is reported to be trying to develop investment links with Israeli interests, with a positive response coming from the plastics industry.[24] Another deal has been concluded by a West German company called Transkei Commercial Productions, under which a German-based factory ship is to have exclusive rights to all fishing off the Transkei coast for ten years in exchange for a royalty of only R30 (£17) per ton — described by a local fishing company as "ridiculously small". An East London lawyer commented: "Do you call this a contract? As far as I'm concerned it is of no value whatsoever. The German company (is in a position) to do what it likes without accountability to the Transkei government."[25] In 1979 a consortium of Swiss banks raised a R7 million (£4m.) loan for the Ciskei, arranged by the British merchant bank Hill Samuel; this loan was guaranteed by the South African government and a similar amount is reported to be being negotiated for BophuthaTswana.[26]

Some "development aid" is also finding its way to the bantustans. Chief Matanzima has boasted of getting technical asssistance from Austria and Taiwan;[27] and Taiwan is also giving aid to QwaQwa.[28] Development experts are starting to turn up at bantustan conferences; at a four-day conference on the Ciskei held in 1978, for example, there were many foreign participants, including Michael Ward from the British government-financed Institute of Development Studies, Joseph Eaton from the University of Pittsburgh, and two delegates from Israel.[29]

The presence of Sir Arthur Snelling on the Ciskei Independence Commission has already been noted; in addition Sir Arthur is also vice-president of the UK-South African Trade Association (UKSATA) one of the major lobbies in Britain urging closer links with South Africa. And the British Council, an agency of the government, has, on occasion, organised tours of development studies centres in Britain for South African academics, for example Prof. Jan Bekker of Zululand University who visited Britain in 1978.[30] One of the aims of such visits appears to be the establishment of 'development studies' courses at the bantustan universities, grafted on to the departments of anthropology, economics or what was formerly known as "native administration", and enjoying foreign support and links with overseas experts in "development". The British government has defended the invitations to South African academics by saying "there is at present no technical co-operation in the usually accepted sense of the phrase (i.e. developmental funds supplied by the Ministry of Overseas Development) between Britain and South Africa."[31] At the same time it is British policy to cultivate links with the black population of South Africa.[32] The implication may be that Britain and other Western countries are moving towards "development aid" for "separate development" in the bantustans of apartheid South Africa.

References

CHAPTER ONE

1. G. J. Joubert and D. Jooste, *History for Standard VII* (Perskor Publishers), p.100.
2. See for example M. Wilson and L. M. Thompson (eds.), *The Oxford History of South Africa*, Vol. I (Oxford University Press, 1969).
3. Quoted in Leo Marquard, *The Story of South Africa*.
4. Wilson and Thompson, *Oxford History*.
5. Randolph Vigne, *The Transkei: South Africa's Tragedy* (The Africa Bureau, London, 1969).
6. C. W. de Kiewiet, *A History of South Africa: Social and Economic* (Cambridge University Press, 1941).
7. Quoted in G. M. Carter, T. Karis and N. M. Stultz, *South Africa's Transkei: The Politics of Domestic Colonialism* (Northwestern University Press, Evanston, Ill., 1967).
8. Report by the Akademie für deutsches Recht submitted to the Ministry of Justice June 1939; quoted in A. Kum's N'dumbe, "Hitler, l'Afrique du Sud et la Menace Imperialiste," *Les Temps Modernes*, Paris, No. 327, October 1973. For further details of the Nazi links with South Africa and Namibia, see N'dumbe's article and Brian Bunting, *The Rise of the South African Reich* (Penguin, London, 1969).
9. Cited in Ivor Wilkins and Hans Strydom, *The Super-Afrikaners: Inside the Afrikaner Broederbond* (Jonathan Ball Publishers, Johannesburg, 1978), p. 193.
10. *Debates*, 12.4.50.
11. *Debates*, 27.1.59.
12. *Debates*, 23.1.62.
13. *Debates*, 10.4.61.
14. Carter *et al*, *Transkei*.
15. *Debates*, 23.1.62.
16. *Report of the Commission for the Socio-Economic Development of the Bantu Areas within the Union of South Africa* (Tomlinson Commission Report) (Government Printer, Pretoria), U.G. 61/1955.
17. *The Star*, Johannesburg, 26.10.74.
18. *Debates*, 22.7.70.
19. *Debates*, 18.6.69.
20. Quoted in Lawrence Schlemmer, *Social Change and Political Policy in South Africa* (Institute of Race Relations, Johannesburg, 1971).
21. *Sunday Times*, Johannesburg, 11.10.70.
22. *The Post*, Johannesburg, 3.3.78.
23. Wilkins and Strydom, *Super-Afrikaners*, p. 204.
24. Dirk Rezelman in *Rand Daily Mail*, Johannesburg, 24.3.76.
25. Quoted in *Rand Daily Mail*, 5.4.75.
26. *Debates*, 9.5.72.
27. *Debates*, 25.4.73, col. 4995.
28. *Sunday Times*, Johannesburg, 13.8.72.
29. *The Star*, 4.5.74. *Rand Daily Mail*, 30. 5.74.
30. *Debates*, 17, 1973, cols. 8136 and 8139.
31. Interview in Sunday Times, Johannesburg, 13.8. 78.
32. *Financial Mail*, Johannesburg, 28.1.79.
33. Dr. Hartzenburg, Deputy Minister of Plural Development, quoted in *Rand Daily Mail*, 23.1.79.
34. *Daily Dispatch*, East London, 8.6.78.
35. *Daily Dispatch*, 8.11.78.
36. *The Star*, Johannesburg, 26.1.79.
37. *Financial Mail*, 26.1.79.
38. *Rand Daily Mail*, 14.9.78, 23.1.79.
39. *Financial Times*, London, 20.9.79.
40. *Sunday Express*, Johannesburg, 16.9.79.
41. *Ibid*.

CHAPTER TWO

1. *Report of the Transvaal Local Government Commission* (Stallard Commission) (Government Printer, Pretoria), T.P.I. 1922.
2. *Debates*, 6.2.67.
3. *Debates*, 24.4.68.
4. *Debates*, 6.2.68.
5. *Rand Daily Mail*, 28.3.69.
6. *The Star*, 28.3.69
7. *Rand Daily Mail*, 28.3.69.
8. *The Star*, 7.3.70.
9. *Debates*, 20.4.72.
10. *Cape Times*, 1.3.78.
11. *Financial Mail*, 29.9.78.
12. *The Star*, Johannesburg, 28.5.77.
13. Ivor Wilkinson and Hans Strydom, *The Super-Afrikaners*, pp. 210-12.
14. *House of Assembly Debates (Hansard)*, 7.2.78, col. 579.
15. See the analysis in *Black Sash National Conference 1978: The New Foreigners* (Black Sash, Johannesburg, 1978. Mimeo.).
16. *Rand Daily Mail-Extra*, 8.1.77.
17. Letter to *Rand Daily Mail*, 22.11.78.
18. Quoted by Prof. Njisane, *Sunday Times*, Johannesburg, 30.1.77.
19. *Financial Mail*, 26.1.79.
20. South African Institute of Race Relations, *A Survey of Race Relations 1977* (SAIRR, Johannesburg, 1978), p. 342.
21. Letter to *Rand Daily Mail*, 22.11.78.
22. *The World*, Johannesburg, 13.2.77.
23. *Ibid.*, 7.3.77.

24. *Ibid.*
25. *The Guardian*, London, 25.7.77.
26. *Rand Daily Mail*, 13.1.75.
27. *Ibid.*, 5.11.77.
28. *The World*, 2.10.77.
29. Peter Brown, "Reflections on Graaff-Reinet," in *Reality*, May 1978, p. 6.
30. *The Star*, weekly edition, 19.1.74.

31. *Rand Daily Mail*, 3.1.76.
32. *The Star*, 6.12.75.
33. *The World*, 30.4.76.
34. *Ibid.*, 17.10.77.
35. *Financial Mail*, 3.3.78.
36. *Daily Dispatch*, East London, 24.2.78.
37. *The World*, 30.4.76.

CHAPTER THREE

1. *Rand Daily Mail*, 16 and 28.3.74.
2. *The Star* weekly, 6.4.74.
3. *South African Digest*, Pretoria, 6.9.74.
4. *SAIRR Survey*, 1974, p. 190.
5. *The Star* weekly, 13.4.74.
6. *Rand Daily Mail*, 8.7.74.
7. *Ibid.*, 22 and 24.8.74.
8. *The World*, 5.2.75.
9. *The Guardian*, 27.10.76.
10. *The Times*, London, 25.10.76.
11. *Ibid.*; and *The Guardian*, 27.10.76.
12. *The Star*, 18.2.78.
13. *Ibid.*
14. *The Times*, 17.4.78
15. *Daily Dispatch*, December 1978 (n.d.).
16. *Rand Daily Mail*, 29.5.78.
17. *The Guardian*, 11.5.78.
18. *The Voice of Transkei: Break with South Africa* (Dept. of Foreign Affairs and Tourism, Umtata, 1978).
19. *Daily News*, Durban, 11.4.78.
20. *The Star*, 29.4.78.
21. David Thomas of the *Daily News* in *The Times*, London, Survey of Transkei, 26.10.78.
22. Minister of Foriegn Affairs, in *Debates*, 3.5.78.
23. *Cape Times*, 22.4.78.
24. *Daily News*, 22.9.78; *Africa Confidential*, London, 8.9.78.
25. *Rand Daily Mail*, 13.10.78.
26. *Ibid.*, 17.2.79.
27. *Daily Dispatch*, 4.12.78.
28. Quoted in Ivor Wilkins and Hans Strydom, *The Super-Afrikaners*, p. 209.
29. *The Star*, 30.12.78.
30. *Rand Daily Mail*, 20.1.78.
31. *Ibid.*, 17.2.79.
32. *Ibid.*, 19.2.79.
33. *Sunday Times*, Johannesburg, 18.2.79.
34. *Cape Times*, 13.2.79.
35. *The World*, 18.7.77.
36. *Sunday Express*, Johannesburg, 13.11.77.
37. *Sunday Times*, 6.8.78.
38. *Ibid.*, 11.12.77.
39. *The Star*, 24.12.77.
40. *Ibid.*
41. *Daily Dispatch*, 22.5.78.
42. *Weekend World*, 24.7.77; *The World*, 14.8.77.
43. Quoted in *The World*, 14.8.77.
44. *Ibid.*
45. *Rand Daily Mail*, 23.7.77.
46. *SAIRR Survey of Race Relations 1977*, p. 334.
47. *The Times*, 7.12.77.

48. Quoted in *Africa*, London, No. 73, September 1977, p. 47.
49. *Ibid.*
50. *Rand Daily Mail*, 6.12.77; *The Observer* magazine, 3.12.78, pp. 49-56; *The Times*, 6.12.77.
51. *The Observer* magazine (supra.)
52. *Rand Daily Mail*, 6.12.77.
53. *Ibid.*
54. *Ibid.*
55. *The Observer* magazine (supra.)
56. *The Star*, 11.2.78.
57. *Sunday Times*, 4.12.77.
58. *Rand Daily Mail*, 14.10.77.
59. *The Times*, 6.12.77; *The World*, 27.9.77.
60. *Rand Daily Mail*, 13.12.77.
61. *Ibid.*, 10.12.77.
62. *The World*, 25.9.77.
63. *Weekend World*, 24.7.77.
64. *The Times*, 7.7.77.
65. Editorial, *Rand Daily Mail*, 2.2.78.
66. *Rand Daily Mail*, 2.7.77.
67. *Sunday Times*, Johannesburg, 6.8.78; *The Post*, Johannesburg, 15.2.78.
68. *The Guardian*, 26.4.78; *Financial Times*, 25.4.78.
69. *The Post*, 10.12.78; *Sunday Times*, 10.9.78.
70. *Rand Daily Mail*, 7.7.78; 12.7.78.
71. *Ibid.*, 27.2.79.
72. *Ibid.*, 12.7.78.
73. *The Observer* magazine, 3.12.78.
74. *Sunday Times*, 11.12.77.
75. *Rand Daily Mail*, 19.12.77; *The Voice*, (Johannesburg) 31.12.77.
76. *The Post*, 5.1.79.
77. *Sunday Times*, 6.8.78.
78. *Rand Daily Mail*, 10.2.78.
79. *The Voice*, 31.12.77.
80. *Rand Daily Mail*, 6.12.77.
81. *The Star*, 3.2.79.
82. *The Post*, 7.8.78.
83. *Rand Daily Mail*, 29.12.78.
84. *New African*, London, October 1979.
85. *Sunday Times*, 12.2.78.
86. *Ibid.*, 22.8.76.
87. *Cape Times*, 27.11.76.
88. *Rand Daily Mail*, 28.3.77.
89. *The Post*, 11.12.77.
90. *Rand Daily Mail*, 14.12.77.
91. Quoted in *Weekend World*, 17.7.77.
92. *Ibid.*
93. *ANC Speaks*, (ANC, 1977) p. 206.

CHAPTER FOUR

1. Muriel Horrell, *The African Homelands of South Africa* (Institute of Race Relations, Johannesburg, 1973), p. 4.
2. SAIRR *Survey of Race Relations*, 1974 p. 181.
3. SAIRR *Survey*, 1972, p. 166.
4. Minister of Bantu Affairs and Development, *Debates* 1977, cols. 596-7.
5. Republic of South Africa, *South African Statistics* 1972. Government Printer, Pretoria), A-13 and A-14.
6. Govan Mbeki; *Transkei: The Peasants' Revolt* (Penguin, 1964), p. 18.
7. *Sunday Tribune*, Johannesburg, 30.4.78.
8. *Bantu*, January, 1972; Christopher R. Hill, *Bantustans: The Fragmentation of South Africa* (Oxford University Press, 1964).
9. Muriel Horrell, *The African Homelands of South Africa* (Institute of Race Relations, Johannesburg, 1973).
10. *Ibid.*
11. *Debates*, 18.6.51.
12. *Bantu*, January, 1972.
13. *Debates*, 7.3.68.
14. *Debates*, 24.2.70., col. 1941.
15. *Bantu*, January, 1972.
16. Horrell, *African Homelands*, p. 14; SAIRR *Survey of Race Relations*, 1973, p. 145.
17. *Government Gazette* (Government Printer, Pretoria), No. 4486, 6.11.74.
18. *Debates*, 14 and 21.10.74; *Government Gazette*, No. 4487, 6.11.74.
19. John Dugard, "The Legal Framework of Apartheid," in *South African Dialogue* (McGraw-Hill, New York, 1972), pp. 98-9.
20. SAIRR *Survey*, 1977, p. 366.

CHAPTER FIVE

1. Minister of Plural Relations and Development, *Debates*, 17.5.78.
2. *New York Times*, 28.9.75.
3. *The Star*, weekly edition, 3.2.73; Survey by Markinor, quoted in *Rand Daily Mail*, 30.11.74.
4. Republic of South Africa, *Tomlinson Commission Report*, U.G. 61/1955 (Government Printer, Pretoria, 1955).
5. *The Star*, 6.6.68.
6. *Rand Daily Mail*, Johannesburg, 30.11.74.
7. Francis Wilson, *Migrant Labour in South Africa* (Spro-cas and the South African Council of Churches, Johannesburg, 1972), p. 102.
8. *The Star*, 12, 16, 23 and 30.12.72.
9. Dr. Trudi Thomas, *New Hope in the Ciskei*, address delivered at the annual general meeting of Kupugani in East London, August 1974.
10. L. Schlemmer and P. Stopforth, *A study of Malnutrition in the Nqutu District of KwaZulu*, Institute for Social Research, Fact Paper No. 2., July 1974.
11. Essop Patel (ed.), *The World of Nat Nakasa: selected writings of the late Nat Nakasa* (Raven Press, Johannesburg, 1975), pp. 47-50.
12. *The Star*, weekly edition, 24.4.71.
13. D. F. Kokot, "Desert Encroachment in South Africa," in Peter R. Gould (ed.), *Africa, Continent of Change* (Belmont, Wadsworth, 1961).
14. Bureau for Economic Research re Bantu Development (Benbo), *QwaQwa* (Johannesburg, 1978).
15. *Rand Daily Mail*, 28.3.68.
16. *The Star*, 2.9.78.
17. *Annual Report, 1978*, quoted in *Cape Times*, 19.12.78.
18. SAIRR *Survey*, 1972, p. 168.
19. *Rand Daily Mail*, 24.3.76.
20. Muriel Horrell, *The African Homelands of South Africa* (Institute of Race Relations, Johannesburg, 1973).
21. *Sechaba*, (ANC), June 1979.
22. *The Star*, 10.6.72.
23. *The Star*, 8.3.72.
24. P. de Briey, "The Productivity of African Labour", in Gould, *Africa*.
25. Republic of South Africa, *South African Statistics*, 1970, pp. J-6, J-8 and J-10.
26. Mr. M. C. Botha in the House of Assembly, quoted in *The Star* weekly, 23.2.74.
27. Merle Lipton, "The South African Census and the Bantustan Policy," *World Today* London, June 1972; *Washington Post*, 4.8.72.
28. Charles Hooper, *Brief Authority* (Collins, London, 1960).
29. *Debates*, 31.1.61 and 20.4.61; *Rand Daily Mail*, 7.7.75.
30. *The Star* weekly, 31.3.73.
31. *Ibid.*
32. *Financial Gazette*, Johannesburg, 20.7.73; *Rand Daily Mail*, 21.7.73.
33. Study by Jeff Leeuwenberg quoted in *Daily Dispatch*, 2.8.78.
34. *Sunday Times*, 10.12.78.
35. *Daily Dispatch*, 16.6.78.
36. For a description of conditions, see Cosmas Desmond, *The Discarded People* (Penguin, London, 1972).
37. Interviews by the author with doctors and nurses in the Transkei, June 1971.
38. See Randolph Vigne, *The Transkei: South Africa's Tragedy* (Africa Bureau, London, 1969).
39. *The Star* weekly, 28.4.73.
40. Interviews by the author in the Transkei, June 1971.
41. *Rand Daily Mail*, 8.8.72.
42. *The Star* weekly, 16.12.72.
43. *Ibid.*, 9.6.73.
44. Interviews by the author in the Transkei, Ciskei and KwaZulu, June-July 1971.
45. *Ibid.*, 19.1.74.
46. *Ibid.*, 4.1.75.
47. *Ibid.*, 5.5.73.
48. *Rand Daily Mail*, 6.10.72.

49. *Ibid.*, 9.5.74.; *The Star*, 14.5.74.
50. *The Star* weekly, 18.8.73 and 8.9.73.
51. *Ibid.*, 15.9.73.
52. *The Star* weekly, 29.12.73.
53. *The World*, Johannesburg, 15.9.74 and 6.10.74.
54. *The World*, 27.9.77.
55. *Cape Times*, 28.9.77.
56. *The World*, 6.10.77.
57. *Daily Dispatch*, 19.10.77.
58. *The Post*, 3-5.11.77.
59. *Rand Daily Mail*, 24.2.78.
60. *Ibid.*, 21.6.78.
61. *Daily Dispatch*, 25.7.78.
62. *Rand Daily Mail*, 6.10.77.
63. *Ibid.*
64. *Cape Argus*, 5.10.77.
65. *Rand Daily Mail*, 5.10.77.
66. *Cape Times*, 20.10.77.
67. *Daily Dispatch*, 3.4.78.
68. *The World*, 18.7.77; *Rand Daily Mail*, 19.7.77.
69. *Rand Daily Mail*, 5.10.77.
70. *Cape Times*, 9.8.77; *The World*, 18.8.77; see also Counter-Information Services, *Black South Africa Explodes* (CIS, London, 1977), pp. 10, 14.
71. *Rand Daily Mail*, 10.8.76.
72. *Ibid.*, 24.7.78.
73. *The World*, 28.8.77.
74. *Weekend World*, 10.7.77.
75. Minister of Police, *Debates*, 20.4.76.
76. *Rand Daily Mail*, 30.12.76.
77. *Ibid.*
78. *Cape Times*, 31.12.76.
79. *Financial Mail*, 16.2.79; see also *Black Sash*, February 1979.
80. *Ibid.*
81. *Ibid.*
82. *Rand Daily Mail*, 14.3.78.
83. *The Post*, 13.8.78.
84. *The Star*, 2.10.76.
85. Mdukutshani newsletter (mimeo.), September 1978.
86. *Rhodesia Herald*, 21.5.77.
87. *Rand Daily Mail*, 25.4.78.
88. *The Post*, 9.7.78.

CHAPTER SIX

1. From an article on the Bantustans printed in *Liberation* in May 1959; reprinted in *Nelson Mandela: The Struggle is My Life* (IDAF, December 1978).
2. *This is Apartheid* (IDAF, 1978), p. 18.
3. United Nations Centre on Apartheid, *The Effects of Apartheid on the Status of Women in South Africa*, Document No. 78-10115.
4. Quoted in Cosmas Desmond, *The Discarded People* (Penguin, London, 1972), p. 14.
5. Alan Baldwin, "Mass Population Removals and Break-up of Family Life in South Africa," Memorandum submitted by the Africa Bureau, London, to the United Nations Special Committee against Apartheid: *Objective; Justice* (United Nations, New York), Vol. 7 No. 1, January/February/March 1975, p. 19.
6. Nelson Mandela: *The Struggle is My Life* (IDAF, 1978), pp. 61-2.
7. Elizabeth S. Landis, *Apartheid and the Disabilities of African Women in South Africa*, United Nations Unit on Apartheid, Notes and Documents No. 4/75, March 1975.
8. Merle Lipton, "The South African Census and the Bantustan Policy," *World Today*, London, June 1972; *Washington Post*, 4.8.72.
9. Charles Hooper, *Brief Authority* (Collins, London, 1960).
10. See e.g. *Survey of Race Relations*, 1972, 1973 and 1974; International Defence and Aid Fund, *Southern African Information Service* (1969-74), "Resettlement," and *Uprooting a Nation* (African Publications Trust, London, 1974).
11. *The Star*, 21.11.69.
12. *Rand Daily Mail*, 13 and 15.6.74.
13. Horrell, *African Homelands*, p. 2.
14. SAIRR *Survey*, 1974. pp. 200-1.
15. *Rand Daily Mail*, 7 and 8.9.73.
16. *Ibid.*, 25.3.75.
17. *The Star* weekly, 9.6.73.
18. *Financial Mail*, Johannesburg, 23.6.72.
19. *The Star* weekly, 3.3.73.
20. *Ibid.*, 4.11.72.
21. *Ibid.*, 5.5.73.
22. Sir de Villiers Graaff, Chairman of the United Party, quoted in ibid., 4.11.72.
23. *Ibid.*, 16.9.72.
24. *Rand Daily Mail*, 8.12.77.
25. Letter to *ibid.*, 23.1.79.
26. *The Guardian*, 26.1.79.
27. *The Voice*, 27.1.79.
28. *The Post*, 22.10.78.
29. *The Voice*, 20.5.78.
30. *The Post*, 18.8.78; 29.10.78; 29.11.78; *Sunday Post*, 22.10.78.
31. *The Post*, 1.12.78.
32. *Sunday Post*, 22.10.78.
33. *Ibid.*
34. *The Post*, 16.10.78.
35. *The Voice*, 27.1.79.
36. *Rand Daily Mail*, 20.12.78.
37. *The Post*, 3.12.78.
38. *Ibid.*, 6.12.78.
39. *Ibid.*, 20.12.78.
40. *Ibid.*, 28.12.78.
41. *Rand Daily Mail*, 9.2.79.
42. *Ibid.*, 10.8.77.
43. *Ibid.*, 15.8.77.
44. *The World*, 14.8.77.
45. *The Post*, 25.1.78; 24.2.78; 13.7.78; 20.12.78.
46. *Rand Daily Mail*, 7.9.78.
47. *The World*, 22.5.77.
48. *The Voice*, 8.4.78.
49. *Ibid.*
50. *Rand Daily Mail*, 18.1.78; *The Voice*, 6.5.78; *The Post*, 22.1.78; 30.4.78.
51. *Rand Daily Mail*, 16.6.76.
52. Cosmas Desmond, *Limehill revisited: a case-study of the longer-term effects of African resettlement*. Development Studies Research Group, Working Paper No. 5 (University of Natal, Pietermaritzburg, Department of Economics, 1978), pp. 4-11, 17.
53. *The Times*, 21.1.77.
54. *Daily Dispatch*, 16.1.69.
55. Christopher R. Hill, *Bantustans: The Fragmentation of South Africa* (Oxford University Press, 1964).
56. *Debates*, 4.2.69.

128

CHAPTER SEVEN

1. *The Star*, 2.11.72.
2. *Rand Daily Mail*, 25.3.75.
3. *Rand Daily Mail*, 26.5.78.
4. *The Post*, 28.5.78.
5. *Daily Dispatch*, 12.5.78.
6. *Rand Daily Mail*, 6.4.74; 18.4.74; 1.5.74; *The Star*, weekly, 20.4.74.
7. *Rand Daily Mail*, 25.3.75.
8. *Ibid.*, 28.12.76.
9. *The Post*, 30.10.78.
10. *The World*, 9.7.77.
11. *Ibid.*, 24.3.77.
12. *Ibid.*
13. *Rand Daily Mail*, 2.9.78.
14. *Ibid.*, 7.8.68; *Debates*, 18.6.68.
15. *The Observer* magazine, 3.12.78.
16. *Windhoek Observer*, 14.10.78.
17. *The Times*, 22.1.76.
18. *Rand Daily Mail*, 5.3.75; 22.3.75; *The Star*, weekly, 10.3.73.
19. *Rand Daily Mail*, 5.7.75.
20. *Ibid.*, 20.3.75.
21. *Ibid.*, 1.3.74; 28.6.74.
22. *Ibid.*, 21.7.73, and 19.9.73; *Financial Times*, London, 19.9.73, and 4.12.73.
23. *The Star*, editorial, 24.1.74.
24. *Rand Daily Mail*, 21.2.75.
25. *The Star* weekly, 18.5.74.
26. *The Star*, 15.11.75.
27. *Rand Daily Mail*, 21.3.78.
28. *Ibid.*, 3.5.78.
29. *The Post*, 16.2.78.
30. *Rand Daily Mail*, 9.1.78.
31. *Ibid.*, 10.4.74.
32. *The Voice*, 18.11.78.
33. *The World*, 24.5.77.
34. *Rand Daily Mail*, 10.1.78.
35. *The Star*, weekly, 13.7.74.
36. *Ibid.*, 12.5.73.
37. Quoted in Ivor Wilkins and Hans Strydom, *The Super-Afrikaners, p. 207.*
38. *Sunday Times*, Johannesburg, 22.1.78.
39. *Rand Daily Mail*, 25.8.78.
40. *The Post*, 15.10.78.
41. *Daily News*, Durban, 22.5.78.
42. *The Post*, 8.10.78.
43. *The World*, 17.4.77.
44. See SAIRR, 1977.
45. Quoted in *The World of Nat Nakasa*, p. 48.
46. *The World*, 24.4.77.
47. *Ibid.*, 26.4.77.
48. *Drum*, October 1977, p. 43.
49. *The Post*, 8.10.78.
50. *Debates*, 14 and 21 October, 1974; *Rand Daily Mail*, 14 August, 1974; *The Star*, 28 August and 19 October, 1974.
51. *Rand Daily Mail*, 14.4.75.
52. *Ibid.*, 11.9.72.
53. *Ibid.*, 14.4.75.
54. *Ibid.*, 25.3.75.
55. *The Star*, 31.3.73.
56. *The World*, 20.7.77.
57. *Ibid.*, 23.8.77.
58. *Ibid.*, 28.8.77; 4.9.78.
59. *Ibid.*, 6.9.77.
60. *Ibid.*, 2.10.77.
61. *Rand Daily Mail*, 17.8.77.
62. *The World*, 12.10.77.
63. *Daily Dispatch*, 16.12.78.
64. *The Post*, 2.1.79.
65. *Ibid.*, 28.12.78.
66. *Rand Daily Mail*, 22.1.79; 24.1.79.
67. *Government Gazette*, 30.9.77; 2.12.77.
68. *Daily Dispatch*, 31.3.78.
69. *Ibid.*, 5.10.77.
70. *Ibid.*, 19.6.78.
71. *Ibid.*, 16.6.78.
72. *Ibid.*, 7.7.78.
73. *Ibid.*, 14.11.78.
74. *Ibid.*, 6.10.78.
75. *Ibid.*, 10.6.78.
76. *Ibid.*, 11.11.78.
77. *The Voice*, 13.1.79; *Daily Dispatch*, 8.9.78.
78. *Daily Dispatch*, 8.8.78; 17.8.78; 6.11.78.
79. *Ibid.*, 11.9.78.
80. *Ibid.*, 28.7.78.
81. *Ibid.*
82. *The World*, 23.9.77.
83. *Daily Dispatch*, 31.10.77.
84. *Ibid.*
85. *Rand Daily Mail*, 7.6.75.
86. *The Post*, 15.11.78.
87. *Rand Daily Mail*, 11.11.77.
88. *The Post*, 5.2.78.
89. *Debates*, 22.5.73; *Rand Daily Mail*, 24 and 26 April, 1973; *The Star* weekly, 21.4.73. and 5.5.73.
90. *The Star* weekly, 11.5.74.
91. *Rand Daily Mail*, 9.5.74; *Cape Times*, 9.5.74.
92. *Rand Daily Mail*, 12.11.73.
93. *Rand Daily Mail*, 31.3.73.
94. *Ibid.*, 17.5.74.
95. *Ibid.*, 24.6.74.
96. *Rand Daily Mail*, 14 and 17 May, 19, 21, 22, 24 and 26 June, 29 August, 1974; *Sunday Times*, Johannesburg, 19.5.74; *Cape Times*, 14, 15 and 17 May, 17 and 21 June, 1974; *The Star*, weekly, 29.8.74.
97. *The Star*, 29.8.74.
98. *Daily Dispatch*, 14.3.78; *The Post*, 14.3.78.
99. *Daily Dispatch*, 14.3.78; *New African*, June 1978, p. 11.
100. *Rand Daily Mail*, 20.4.78.
101. *The World*, 15.5.77.
102. *Daily Dispatch*, 11.5.78.
103. *Rand Daily Mail*, 4.5.78.
104. *Cape Times*, 10.8.76.
105. *SAIRR Survey*, 1973, p. 161; *SAIRR Survey*, 1974, p. 202; *Rand Daily Mail*, 6, 12, 13, 16, 21 and 23 March, 2, 12, 17 and 25 April, 2 and 4 May, 4 June, 1974; *Cape Times*, 5 and 9 March, 1974; *The Star* weekly, 30 March, 6 and 13 April, 1974.
106. *Rand Daily Mail*, 29.7.75; 2.8.75.
107. *Ibid.*, 21.3.75.
108. *The Post*, 5.1.78.
109. *Ibid.*, 13.8.78.
110. *Ibid.*, 12.2.78.
111. *Rand Daily Mail*, 26.7.75.
112. *Ibid.*, 2.9.77; *The Post*, 12.12.77.
113. *The Star*, 2.12.78.
114. *The World*, 11.2.75; *SAIRR Survey*, 1974, p. 214; *The Star*, 2.4.75; *Rand Daily Mail*, 20.6.75.

115. *The Post*, 1.3.78.
116. *Ibid.*, 11.4.78.
117. *Government Gazette* 6217, 17.11.78.
118. Randolph Vigne, *The Transkei: South Africa's Tragedy* (Africa Bureau, London, 1969).
119. G. M. Carter, T. Karis and N. M. Stultz, *South Africa's Transkei: The Politics of Domestic Colonialism*.
120. Vigne, *Transkei. op. cit.*
121. *Evening Post*, Port Elizabeth, 8.11.63; *Daily Dispatch*, East London, 18.11.63.
122. Vigne, *Transkei*.
123. Vigne, *Transkei*; M. Wilson and L. M. Thompson, eds., *The Oxford History of South Africa*, Vol. I.
124. *Newsletter*, SAIRR, March 1969.
125. *Rand Daily Mail*, 1.11.68.
126. *Ibid.*, 23.4.71.
127. *Ibid.*, 8.11.68.
128. *Financial Gazette*, Johannesburg , 9 November, 1973; *The Star* weekly, 27 October and 24 November, 1973; *Cape Times*, 2 August, 5 September, 26 October, 3 November, 1973; *Sunday Times* Johannesburg, 22 July and 7 October, 1973; *Rand Daily Mail*, 24 July, 29 August, 3 and 10 November, 1973.
129. *The Star* weekly, 23.3.74.
130. *Rand Daily Mail*, 8.8.74.
131. Quoted in *The Guardian*, 26.10.76.
132. *Africa* No. 73, September 1977, p. 48.
133. SAIRR *Survey*, 1977.
134. *Daily Dispatch*, 8.12.78; *Rand Daily Mail*, 26.8.78; *The Post*, 25.8.78.
135. *Daily Dispatch*, 5.7.78; *The Star*, 24.6.78.
136. *Rand Daily Mail*, 27.5.78.
137. *The Guardian*, 13.1.78.
138. See SAIRR *Survey*, 1977, pp. 167-68.
139. *Daily Dispatch*, 29.3.78.
140. *The Voice*, 21.10.78.
141. *Daily Dispatch*, 20.12.78.
142. *The Post*, 11.6.78.
143. *Daily Dispatch*, 26.8.78.
144. *Ibid.*, 7.7.78.
145. *Ibid.*, 21.3.78.
146. *Rand Daily Mail*, 27 and 28 July, 6, 15, 16, 17, 25 and 29 August, 1 September, 19 October, 1973; 30 January, 14, 15, 18, 20 and 29 March, 9 and 15 April, 7 and 29 May, 25 July, 9 August, 1974; *The Star* weekly, 1 September, 20 and 27 October, 1973; 23 March, 1974; *Cape Times*, 16, 29 and 30 August, 1973; 14 and 20 March, 1974.
147. *Rand Daily Mail*, 23.5.78.
148. *Daily Dispatch*, 21.10.78.
149. *Rand Daily Mail*, 22.7.78.
150. *Ibid.*
151. *The Guardian*, 24.7.78.
152. *The Voice*, 26.7.78.
153. *Daily Dispatch*, 8.9.78.
154. *Sunday Express*, Johannesburg, 17.9.78.
155. *New African*, October 1979.
156. Horrell, *African Homelands*, p. 40.
157. Chief Ntunja Mngomezulu, quoted in *The World*, 14.6.77.
158. *Ibid.*
159. Hector Bongani Ncokazi, chapter in *Transkei Independence*, Black Viewpoint No. 4 (Black Community Programmes, Durban, 1976), pp. 20-21.
160. Quoted in *The World*, 15.8.77.
161. Vigne, *Transkei*.
162. *Cape Times*, 17.10.75; 29.1.77.
163. *Rand Daily Mail*, 25.3.77.
164. *Rand Daily Mail*, 20.3.78; *The Star*, 4.2.78; Eduard Abel in *Lutheran World Federation Information*, 17/78, 18.4.78.
165. *The Post*, 26.4.78.
166. *The Star*, 20.10.71.
167. *The Star* weekly, 18.5.74.
168. *The World*, 11.3.74.
169. *Rand Daily Mail*, 30.11.72.
170. *The Star* weekly, 29 September, 1973; *The Star*, 5 and 7 July, 15 and 16 September, 1972; *Rand Daily Mail*, 6 July, 15 and 17 September, 1972.
171. *Rand Daily Mail*, 14.10.77.
172. *The Post*, 23.1.78.
173. *The Star*, 1.11.74.
174. *Rand Daily Mail*, 16.2.73.
175. *Sunday Times*, Johannesburg, 13.8.72.
176. *Ibid.*, 13.1.75.
177. *The Star* weekly, 18.5.74.
178. *The Star*, 13.7.74.
179. *The Star* weekly, 19.5.73.
180. Markinor survey, quoted in *Rand Daily Mail*, 2.12.74.
181. *SASO Newsletter*, September/October, 1972.
182. *The Guardian*, London, 18.11.74.
183. *Cape Times*, 28.3.75.
184. *The Voice*, 8.4.78.
185. *Rand Daily Mail*, 5, 9, 11 and 18 November, 1973; *The Star* weekly, 16.11.73 and 19.1.74.
186. *The Star* weekly, 9.3.74; *Sunday Times*, Johannesburg, 10.3.74.
187. *The Star*, 10.12.77.
188. *Rand Daily Mail*, 27.1.79.
189. *The Post*, 10.2.78.
190. *Rand Daily Mail*, 26.2.79.

CHAPTER EIGHT

1. *Daily Dispatch*, 16.5.78.
2. *The Post*, 3-5.11.77.
3. *Ibid.*, 28.5.78; *Rand Daily Mail* 26.5.78.
4. *Debates*, 26.4.76
5. *Ibid.*
6. *The Star*, weekly, 20.1.73.
7. *Sunday Times*, Johannesburg, 11.2.79.
8. *Daily Dispatch*, 20.3.78.
9. *Financial Mail*, 27.3.75; *The Star*, 27.3.75.
10. Cosmas Desmond, *The Discarded People* (Penguin, London, 1972), Appendix II.
11. *Ibid.*
12. G. M. Carter, T. Karis and N. M. Stultz, *South Africa's Transkei: The Politics of Domestic Colonialism*.
13. *Debates*, 18.5.67.
14. *The Star*, 19.5.67.
15. *Debates*, 24.2.69.
16. SAIRR *Survey*. pp. 185-6.
17. Mr. M. J. Nduba, quoted in *The Post*, 13.9.78.
18. *Transkei Government Gazette* No. 44, 28.7.78.
19. SAIRR *Survey*, 1977, pp. 337-8.

20. *Rand Daily Mail*, 6.9.77.
21. *Daily Dispatch*, 29.10.77; 31.9.78.
22. *Rand Daily Mail*, 28.3.77; *The Post*, 16.6.78.
23. *Financial Times*, 10.5.78.
24. *Financial Mail*, 11.8.78.
25. *Ibid.*
26. *Financial Times*, 10.5.78.
27. *Financial Mail*, 11.8.78.
28. *The Post*, 12.10.78.
29. *Ibid.*, 10.12.78.
30. *Sunday Express*, London, 17.9.78.
31. *The Citizen*, Johannesburg, 20.4.78.
32. *Sunday Post*, n.d.
33. *Rand Daily Mail*, 9.1.78.
34. *Government Gazette* 5930, 15.3.78.
35. Muriel Horrell, *The African Homelands of South Africa*, p.7.
36. *The Star*, 26.1.74.
37. *Cape Times*, Cape Town, 20.12.74.
38. *Sunday Tribune*, Johannesburg, 1.9.74.
39. *The Star* weekly 31.3.73.
40. *Daily News*, Johannesburg, 13.9.74; *The Star* weekly, 21.9.74.
41. *The Star* weekly, 9.11.74; *Rand Daily Mail*, 7.2.75.
42. *Rand Daily Mail*, 12.2.75.
43. T. G. Hughes in *Debates*, 11.3.68; *The Star*, 15.7.72; *Rand Daily Mail*, 7.9.74.
44. *Rand Daily Mail*, 21.7.75; *Financial Gazette*, 9.1.76.
45. *The Post*, 13.2.78; *Daily Dispatch*, 11.2.78.
46. *Daily Dispatch*, 24.5.78.
47. *Ibid.*, 16.5.78.
48. Annual Report of the Xhosa Development Corporation for 1967-8, quoted in *The Star*, 10.4.69.
49. *Financial Mail*, 15.12.67.
50. *Rand Daily Mail*, 7.9.74.
51. Muriel Horrell, *South Africa: Basic Facts and Figures* (SAIRR, Johannesburg, 1973), p.40.
52. Horrell, *African Homelands*, pp.59–60.
53. Clarke and Ngobese, *Women without Men*, p.14.
54. *The World*, Johannesburg, 22.3.72.
55. Gillian Hart, *Some Socio-Economic Aspects of African Entrepreneurship* (Institute of Social and Economic Research, University of Rhodes, 1972).
56. *Rand Daily Mail*, 14.12.73.
57. *Rand Daily Mail*, 2.8.75.
58. Prof. H. Houghton in W. Backer, ed., *The Economic Development of the Transkei* (Lovedale Press, Lovedale, 1970); also Merle Lipton, "The South African Census and the Bantustan Policy," *The World Today*, London, June 1972.
59. *The Star* weekly, 21.12.74.
60. *The Star* weekly, 11 and 18 August, 1973.
61. *Debates*, 19.3.68.
62. *The Post*, 24.2.78.
63. *Rhodesian Financial Gazette*, 22.10.76.
64. *Sunday Times*, Johannesburg, 18.9.77.
65. *Rand Daily Mail*, 24.6.78; *Financial Mail*, 30.6.78.
66. *The Times*, supplement on Transkei, 26.10.78.
67. *Sunday Times*, Johannesburg, 15.10.78.
68. *The Times*, supplement. 26.10.78
69. *Sunday Times*, 22.8.76.
70. SAIRR *Survey*, 1976, p.224.

71. *Rand Daily Mail*, 7.10.77; *Weekend World*, 16.10.77.
72. *The Post*, 29.10.78; 6.11.78.
73. *Sunday Times*, 19.11.78.
74. *Ibid.*, 4.6.78.
75. *Financial Mail*, 4.3.77.
76. *Ibid.*, 18.2.77.
77. *Daily Dispatch*, 24.5.78.
78. *Ibid.*, 7.9.78.
79. *Ibid.*, n.d.
80. CED Annual Report, quoted in *Cape Times*, 19.12.78.
81. *The Star* weekly, 26.1.74; *The Homelands: The Role of the Corporations* (Chris van Rensburg Publications, Johannesburg, 1974).
82. *Financial Mail*, 25.10.74.
83. *Rand Daily Mail*, 5 and 18 October, 1974.
84. *Sunday Times*, 24.7.77; 31.7.77.
85. *The Star*, weekly, 21.12.74.
86. *Ibid.*, 11.8.73; 18.8.73.
87. *Daily Dispatch*, 12.11.77.
88. *Ibid.*, 18.9.78.
89. *Rand Daily Mail*, 14.9.78.
90. *The Post*, 4.8.78.
91. *Rand Daily Mail*, 18.9.75.
92. *Financial Mail*, 16.2.79.
93. *Ibid.*, 16.6.78.
94. *Sunday Times*, 17.12.78.
95. Mdukutshani newsletter, August 1978, p.2.
96. CED Annual Report, quoted in *Rand Daily Mail*, 13.12.78.
97. Mr. M. C. Botha speaking at Butterworth, Transkei, quoted in *The Star*, 30.9.71.
98. *Debates*, 29.6.59.
99. Prof. Lombard, *Background to Planning the Development of Bantu Homelands in South Africa*, paper presented to the Conference on Accelerated Development in Southern Africa, Africa Institute, Johannesburg, March 1972.
100. *Ibid.*
101. *Sunday Times*, Johannesburg, 1.3.70.
102. Conclusion of the conference, "Towards a Comprehensive Development in Zululand," Institute for Social Research, University of Natal, February 1971, quoted in *The Star*, 1.3.71.
103. *Financial Gazette*, Johannesburg, 4.12.70.
104. *Ibid.*, 7.6.74.
105. Col. G. H. Boerstra, President of the Northern Transvaal Chamber of Industries, quoted in *The Star* weekly, 2.12.72.
106. *Financial Mail*, 17.3.78.
107. *Rand Daily Mail*, 27.3.73; *Financial Mail*, 13.4.73.
108. *The Star*, 19.1.74; *Financial Mail*, 1.2.74; *Financial Gazette*, 30.5.75.
109. *Financial Mail*, 28.11.69.
110. *The Star*, 21.11.69.
111. *Financial Mail*, 24.8.73.
112. *Financial Mail*, 24.11.78.
113. *To The Point*, Amsterdam, 25.1.74.
114. Minister of Plural Relations, *Debates*, 1.3.78.
115. *Rand Daily Mail*, 14.4.76.
116. *The Star*, weekly, 17.9.77.
117. *The Post*, 11.1.79.
118. *Ibid.*
119. *The Star*, 8.6.74.
120. Prof. H. J. Reynders of Pretoria University, quoted in *Rand Daily Mail*, 18.5.71.

131

121. *Financial Mail*, 11.10.74. and 20.5.71.
122. Witwatersrand branch, NUSAS Wages Commission, quoted in *The Star* weekly, 14.12.74.
123. *Rand Daily Mail*, 30.3.76.
124. CED advertisement in *Sunday Times*, 26.2.78.
125. See United Nations Centre on Apartheid, *The Effects of Apartheid on the Status of Women in South Africa*, Document No. 78-10115.
126. *Financial Mail*, 5.1.79.
127. *Rand Daily Mail*, 7.12.76.
128. *The Post*, 31.12.78.
129. Quoted in Murial Horrell, *South Africa's Workers* (Institute of Race Relations, Johannesburg, 1969), p.42.
130. *Financial Mail*, 4.9.70.
131. Dr. P. J. Riekert, *The Economy of the Republic*, paper given at the Fourth Annual Council Meeting of the Institute of Race Relations, Cape Town, 28-30, 1.70.
132. Letter to Rev. Don Morton from Mr. R. C. Gerstenburg, Chairman, General Motors Corporation, regarding purchases of platinum from South Africa; quoted in U.S. Congress House of Representatives, Committee on Foreign Affairs, (Sub-committee on Africa), *U.S. Business Involvement in Southern Africa*, Part III, p.151.
133. John Laurence, *The Seeds of Disaster* (Gollancz, London, 1968).
134. *The Star*, 12.4.75; *The Star* weekly 19.1.74.
135. Horrell, *African Homelands; Rand Daily Mail*, 9.7.69.
136. *Debates*, 7.2.69.
137. Mr. R. M. Cadman, *Debates*, 31.3.77.
138. *Rand Daily Mail*, 10.4.74.

139. *South African Gazette*, 12.7.74.
140. *Sunday Express*, Johannesburg, 14.12.77.
141. *Rand Daily Mail*, 26.6.78.
142. *Ibid.*
143. *Sunday Times*, n.d.
144. *Ibid.*, 11.2.79.
145. Prof. Lombard, *Background to Planning the Development of Bantu Homelands in South Africa*, paper presented to the Conference on Accelerated Development in Southern Africa, Africa Institute, Johannesburg, March 1972.
146. Statement by Dr. J. Adendorff, quoted in *The Friend*, 30.4.74.
147. *Financial Mail*, 7.9.73.
148. Mr. M. C. Botha in *Debates*, 20.2.68.
149. *Financial Mail*, 8.6.73.
150. John Sackur in *The Times*, London, 27.4.71.
151. Mr. F. Van Wyk, Director of the Institute of Race Relations, quoted in *Rand Daily Mail*, 7.5.71.
152. *The Star*, weekly, 7.12.74.
153. Quoted in *Daily Dispatch*, 2.8.78.
154. *Financial Mail*, 26.1.79.
155. *The Star*, 6.5.78.
156. Sheena Duncan, quoted in *ibid.*, 28.5.77.
157. Pierre van den Berghe, *South Africa, A Study in Conflict* (University of California Press, Berkeley, 1970), pp. 188-9.
158. Lombard and v.d. Merwe in *Finance and Trade Review*, June 1972.
159. *The World*, Johannesburg, 18.7.74.
160. Study by Prof. Piek, quoted in *The Star*, 29.6.74.
161. *Rand Daily Mail*, 18.8.73.
162. *Debates*, 29.6.59, col. 9432.

CHAPTER NINE

1. From information supplied by Haringey Anti-Apartheid Group, London, 1978.
2. *The Emerging States in South Africa*, available from Barclays Bank.
3. *Financial Mail*, 30.6.78.
4. See for example Mr. P. T. du Plessis at the Transvaal National Party Congress, quoted in *Rand Daily Mail*, 14.9.77; and Dr. Breytenbach writing in *Bantu*, July 1977.
5. *Daily Dispatch* 27.10.78.
6. *Ibid.*
7. *Daily Dispatch*, 25.8.78.
8. *Rand Daily Mail*, 14.12.77.
9. *Daily News*, 18.2.78.
10. *Ibid.*
11. *The Star*, 13.10.77; *The Post*, 24.11.77.
12. SAIRR *Survey*, 1977, p.348.
13. *Africa Confidential*, 17.11.78.
14. SAIRR *Survey*, 1977, p.335.
15. *African Business*, December 1978.
16. *The Guardian*, 15.10.77.

17. *Rand Daily Mail*, 21.8.78.
18. *Ibid.*, 27.11.76, 29.11.76.
19. *Daily Dispatch*, 5.12.78.
20. *The Star*, 29.7.78.
21. *Daily Dispatch*, 31.10.78.
22. *Ibid.*, 2.11.78.
23. *Cape Times*, 23.8.78; *The Star*, 26.8.78; *Africa Confidential*, 17.11.78.
24. *The Star*, 26.2.77.
25. *Daily News*, 15.2.78.
26. *Financial Mail*, 19.1.79; *Cape Times*, 2.10.78.
27. *Daily Dispatch*, 1.12.78.
28. *SABC* broadcast 12.7.77.
29. *Daily Dispatch*, 11.5.78; *Rand Daily Mail*, 27.5.78.
30. *The Guardian*, 5.9.78.
31. Letter from Parliamentary Under Secretary of State, Foreign and Commonwealth Office, London, 12.10.78.
32. *The Times*, 28.10.78.

Bibliography

South African Institute of Race Relations, *The African Homelands of South Africa, July 1975–June 1978: a supplementary list of the material held by the Jan H. Hofeyr Library* (SAIRR, Johannesburg, 1978).

South African Institute of Race Relations, annual *Survey of Race Relations.*

International Defence and Aid Fund for Southern Africa, *BophuthaTswana: South Africa's Second 'Independent' Bantustan.* (IDAF Fact Paper on Southern Africa No. 4. November 1977.)

Transkei Independence, Black Viewpoint No. 4 (Durban: Black Community Programmes, 1976).

David M. Smith (ed.), *Separation in South Africa. 2: Homelands and cities.* (Occasional paper, 7. London University, 1976).

Jeffrey Butler, Robert I. Rotberg and John Adams, *The Black Homelands of South Africa: the political and economic development of BophuthaTswana and KwaZulu.* Perspectives on Southern Africa, 21. (Berkeley: University of California Press, 1977.)

Surveys of each bantustan by the Bureau of Economic Research re Bantu Development (Benbo).

Index

Printed in England by A G Bishop & Sons Ltd, Orpington, Kent.